Renal Diet
Cookbook

A COMPLETE GUIDE WITH 200 RECIPES FOR STAGES 3 AND 4 OF CKD "CHRONIC KIDNEY DISEASE."

Stephanie Rice & William Buckley

KW-328-157

Copyright - 2020 - All rights reserved.

The content contained within this book may not be reproduced, duplicated or transmitted without direct written permission from the author or the publisher. Under no circumstances will any blame or legal responsibility be held against the publisher, or author, for any damages, reparation, or monetary loss due to the information contained within this book. Either directly or indirectly.

Legal Notice:

This book is copyright protected. This book is only for personal use. You cannot amend, distribute, sell, use, quote or paraphrase any part, or the content within this book, without the consent of the author or publisher.

Disclaimer Notice:

Please note the information contained within this document is for educational and entertainment purposes only. All effort has been executed to present accurate, up to date, and reliable, complete information. No warranties of any kind are declared or implied. Readers acknowledge that the author is not engaging in the rendering of legal, financial, medical or professional advice. The content within this book has been derived from various sources. Please consult a licensed professional before attempting any techniques outlined in this book.

By reading this document, the reader agrees that under no circumstances is the author responsible for any losses, direct or indirect, which are incurred as a result of the use of information contained within this document, including, but not limited to, - errors, omissions, or inaccuracies.

TABLE OF CONTENTS

CHAPTER 10
Vegetables

CHAPTER 1

What is Meant by Chronic Kidney Disease?

A long-term illness where the kidneys do not function as efficiently as possible is chronic kidney disease (CKD).

Sometimes correlated to being older, it's a normal disorder. It may influence anybody, but it is more prominent in people of black or South Asian heritage.

With time, CKD may grow worse, and finally, the kidneys can stop functioning entirely, although this is unlikely. Most persons with CKD can cope with the disease for a long time.

1.1 Stages of CKD

The kidneys don't normally malfunction all at once in severe kidney disorder. Instead, kidney failure frequently develops steadily in many years. This is good news because medications and behavioral improvements can help delay CKD development are caught early and keep you at your best for as much as possible.

Five Chronic Kidney Disorder Stages

The National Kidney Foundation (NKF) developed a checklist to help physicians recognize kidney disease levels to increase the standard of treatment for people with kidney disease. Kidney disease has been categorized into five stages by the NKF. They will have the right care because the doctor understands what level of kidney failure a person has when each stage needs multiple testing and therapies.

1.2 Glomerular Filtration Level (GFR)

The strongest indicator of kidney activity is the (GFR). The GFR is the figure used to work out the stage of kidney failure of an individual. To measure a GFR, a mathematical method using the person's age, ethnicity, gender, and serum creatinine is used. A blood examination is prescribed by a specialist to determine the amount of serum creatinine. Creatinine is a waste product that originates from the function of muscles. Creatinine is extracted from the blood since the kidneys perform properly. Creatinine amounts in the blood increase as kidney activity decreases.

The five phases of CKD (chronic kidney disease) and GFR (glomerular filtration rate) for each point are demonstrated below:

Stage 5 Final Stage (GFR < 15 mL / min)

Stage 4 Severe kidney disorder (GFR = 15-29 mL / min)

Stage 3B Moderate kidney disorder (GFR = 30-44 mL / min)

Stage 3A Moderate kidney disorder (GFR = 45-59 mL / min)

Stage 2 mild kidney disorder (GFR = 60-89 mL / min)

Stage 1 elevated or average GFR (GFR > 90 mL / min)

CHAPTER 2

Chronic Level 3 Kidney Failure

As CKD is graded into five distinct phases, the best function is indicated in stage 1, and kidney dysfunction is indicated in stage 5. Kidney failure in stage 3 drops straight into the center of the scale. The kidneys have minor to moderate damage at this point.

A specialist can diagnose stage 3 kidney disease depending on the signs as well as testing outcomes. Although you can't restore kidney injury at this point, you can help stop deteriorating damage.

CKD stage 3 is detected based on readings of the estimated glomerular filtration rate (eGFR). It is a blood examination that tests the amounts of creatine. An eGFR is used to assess how effectively the kidneys act to remove waste.

The optimum eGFR is greater than 90, whereas stage 5 CKD is lower than 15 eGFR. So, the greater the eGFR, the better the expected output of your kidney.

Stage 3 CKD comprises two subtypes dependent on eGFR readings. When your eGFR is between 45 and 59, you might be diagnosed with stage 3a. Step 3b means that between 30 and 44 is the eGFR.

For stage 3 CKD, the aim is to stop more deterioration of kidney function. In clinical words, this may signify the avoidance of an eGFR between 29 and 15, which suggests stage 4 CKD.

2.1 Symptoms in stage 3 Kidney disorder

In stages 1 and 2, you do not notice serious kidney disorders, although, in stage 3, the signs appear to become more apparent.

Some of the symptoms of stage 3 of CKD might include:

- Dark red, orange, or yellow urine
- Urinating often or less than average,
- Fluid retention

- Unexplained weariness
- Weakness and other signs close to anemics
- Sleeplessness and other night disorders
- Pain in the lower back
- Blood Pressure Raised

2.2 When to consult a specialist with CKD stage

When you have some of the above signs, it's best to see a physician right away. Although these signs are not exclusive to CKD, it concerns to have any mixture of these symptoms.

If you've recently been classified with stage 1 or stage 2 CKD, you can follow up with your specialist.

Still, you do not have any prior history of CKD until you have been diagnosed with stage 3. This may be linked to the fact that no visible signs are usually induced in phases 1 and 2.

A specialist will administer these checks to detect CKD level 3:

- Readings on blood pressure
- Checks for urine
- EGFR checks (done after the initial diagnosis every 90 days)
- Imaging checks to null out more sophisticated CKD tests

2.3 Therapy for Stage 3 kidney disease

It is unlikely to eradicate kidney disease, but stage 3 means that you do have a possibility to avoid further development of kidney failure. At this point, care and lifestyle modifications are necessary. Your doctor will explore the usage of a mixture of the above therapeutic interventions with you.

Medical therapy

Stage 3 CKD needs no dialysis and no kidney transplant. Instead, such drugs may be administered to you to manage underlying medical problems that can lead to kidney injury.

That involves angiotensin transforming enzyme (ACE) receptors and angiotensin II receptor blockers (ARBs) for elevated blood pressure and glucose regulation for diabetes.

To help ease the side effects of CKD, your doctor can even recommend medicines such as:

- Iron Anemia Supplements
- To avoid bone breaks, calcium, and vitamin D supplements.
- Drugs that minimize cholesterol
- Diuretics for edema care

2.4 Lifestyle Improvements in stage 3 kidney disease patient

Apart from taking the prescription drugs and eating a balanced diet, you will better control CKD stage 3 by making other lifestyle improvements. Speak to the doctor regarding the following things:

- The exercise. For certain days of the week, strive for an average of 30 minutes of moderate exercise each day. A physician will help you safely launch a workout regimen.
- Management of blood pressure. High blood pressure, which will make the disease worse, can be a precursor to CKD. Target a blood pressure of 140/90 or below.
- Managing tension. Techniques may involve fitness, better sleep, and breathing exercises.
- Cessation of Smoking. Speak to a psychiatrist regarding the best smoking prevention approaches for you.

2.5 Could kidney disease stage 3 be reversed?

The aim of stage 3 therapy for CKD is to avoid further development. For either level of CKD, there's no treatment, and you can't undo kidney damage.

However, if you're in stage 3, more harm may also be reduced. Progression in phases 4 and 5 is more challenging to avoid.

2.6 Life expectancy with Level 3 kidney failure

Stage 3 CKD has a better life span than other advanced forms of kidney failure when detected and treated early. Based on age or lifestyle, projections can differ.

One such calculation suggests that in men 40, the average lifespan is 24 years, and 28 in women in the same age range.

It is necessary to understand your probability of disease development, apart from total life expectancy. One 10-year Trusted Source review of patients with stage 3 CKD showed that approximately half advanced to more final kidney disease stages.

Complications with CKD, such as coronary disease, can also be encountered and affect the average life span.

2.6 The Takeaway

When a person begins having signs of this disorder, stage 3 CKD is also first identified.

Although CKD stage 3 is not curable, an earlier diagnosis can indicate a stop to further development. A reduced chance of risks, such as cardiac failure, bone fractures, and anemia, may also be implied.

Getting stage 3 CKD doesn't mean that the disease can lead to kidney failure immediately. It's possible to keep kidney failure from progressing by consulting with a specialist and keeping on top of lifestyle improvements.

CHAPTER 3

What is Kidney Failure Stage 4?

Early-stage progressive kidney failure is considered stage 1 and stage 2. The kidneys are not functioning at 100%, but they are still working well enough that you do not have any signs.

You also lost around half of the kidney capacity by stage 3, contributing to more extreme complications. You have serious, permanent harm to the kidneys in stage 4. However, to slow or stop kidney failure development, there are precautions you should take now.

If you have stage 4 kidney disease, it indicates that the kidneys have been seriously impaired. You have a 15-29 ml/min glomerular filtration volume, or GFR. This is the sum of blood that can be filtered every minute by your kidneys.

GFR could not be correct under cases such as the following:

- Muscular built
- Obesity
- Overweight
- Pregnancy

Other tests that assist in deciding the stage are:

- Glucose levels in the blood
- Urine screening to check at the existence of protein or blood
- Blood testing, to search for other waste materials
- The pressure level in the blood
- Imaging studies to verify the kidney function

Stage 4 is the final stage of kidney disease before kidney failure or stage 5 kidney disorder.

3.1 Symptoms of CKD, stage 4?

Symptoms in stage 4 can include:

- Retention of fluid
- Exhaustion
- Pain in the lower back
- Sleep issues
- Increase in urination and red or dark-looking urine

3.2 Risks of CKD stage 4

1. Fluid retention, which can include:

- Arms and leg swelling (edema)
- High pressure in the blood (hypertension)
- Fluid in the lungs (pulmonary edema)
- It will influence your heart's capacity to work if your potassium levels get too strong (hyperkalemia).

2. Other likely problems are:

- Complications with the heart and blood vessels (Cardiovascular)
- Membrane inflammation around the heart (pericardium)
- High-cholesterol levels
- Low count of red blood cells (anemia)
- Malnourishment
- Bones get weak
- Erectile dysfunction, lowered fertility, decreased drive towards sex
- Difficulty focusing, seizures, and shifts in personality related to central nervous system damage
- Infection weakness owing to a compromised immune response
- If you are pregnant, you and your baby could be at higher risk for kidney failure.

3.3 Therapy for stage 4 kidney disease?

Monitoring and prescribing

You will also visit a kidney doctor (nephrologist) at stage 4 of kidney failure, typically once every 3 months, to control your health. Your blood levels will be tested to check kidney function,

- Calcium
- Bicarbonate
- Creatinine
- Hemoglobin
- Phosphorus
- Potassium

Some routine checks would include:

- Protein in the urine,
- Pressure of blood
- Status of fluid

Your specialist will have you examined for:

- Cardiovascular danger
- Status of Immunization
- Established medicines

3.4 Slowing the development

There is no solution, but there are interventions that may delay development. This includes control and handling of situations such as:

- Anemia
- Bones disorder
- Diabetes
- Edema
- High-cholesterol levels
- Low blood pressure

To help avoid kidney failure and heart disease, it's crucial to consider all your drugs as prescribed.

3.5 Lifestyle Improvements in Stage 4 Kidney Disorder

Several lifestyle improvements can avoid more harm to kidneys. This involves the following:

- No smoking. Smoking is harmful to blood circulation and the lungs. It raises the likelihood of coagulation, heart disease, and stroke. Speak to a health care professional about smoke prevention services if you have problems stopping.

- Exercise. Plan to workout 30 minutes a day, at least five days a week.

- Taking all prescription drugs as instructed. In addition to following all prescription drugs, inform the health care professional before introducing some over-the-counter (OTC) medications or supplements.

- See a primary care physician daily. Please make sure to track and resolve your recent and deteriorating symptoms with your healthcare professional.

3.6 Diagnosis and treatment for stage 4 kidney disease

There is no treatment for stage 4 progressive kidney disorder. Care aims to avoid renal failure and preserve a healthy standard of life.

In 2012, researchers noticed that men and women with poor renal function, particularly less than 30%, had dramatically reduced life expectancy.

They noticed that women appear to have a greater life expectancy at all levels of kidney disease, bar stage 4, where there is just a small gender gap. With age, the prognosis appears to worsen.

About 40 years of age, lifespan is around 10.4 years for men and 9.1 years for women.

At 60 years of age, lifespan is roughly 5.6 years for men and 6.2 years for women.

At 80 years of age, lifespan is roughly 2.5 years for men and 3.1 years for women.

Your specific prognosis often relies on the circumstances under which you coexist and what medications you undergo. Your healthcare professional will offer you a clearer sense of what to expect from you.

3.7 The take-away

Stage 4 renal failure is a critical illness. Careful supervision and treatment can help slow down the process and possibly avoid kidney disease.

At the present rate, it is necessary to brace for dialysis or kidney transplantation in the occurrence of kidney failure.

Treatment includes the control of coexisting clinical problems and compassionate services. It's important to visit a kidney doctor daily to track your health and delay disease development.

CHAPTER 4

Is Nutrition Essential for People with CKD?

An individual can delay or prevent some of the health problems caused by CKD by consuming the right nutrient foods and limiting foods high in potassium, sodium, and phosphorus. For an individual with advanced CKD, knowing about proteins, fats, fluids, and calories is essential. Protein Ingredients, such as dairy products and beef, break down into excess products extracted through the blood by healthy kidneys. That's why limiting these items in your eating habits is essential.

Nutritional requirements change as CKD advances. The health care professional can suggest that a person with impaired kidney function select the food carefully.

4.1 Stage 3 CKD diet

Processed goods are particularly difficult for the body. Because your kidneys are responsible for eliminating waste and managing electrolytes, consuming so much of the wrong foods will overwhelm your kidneys.

It is necessary to consume more whole foods, such as produce and grains, and to consume less refined foods and less saturated fats contained in animal products.

Your doctor can suggest lowering your protein consumption. They can also suggest avoiding such high-potassium foods such as bananas, potatoes, and tomatoes if the potassium values are too high because of CKD.

The same idea refers to sodium. You will need to minimize salty foods if the sodium values are too high.

Weight loss is normal in more advanced phases of CKD owing to loss of appetite. This can even place you at the stake of malnutrition.

If you're feeling a lack of appetite, try consuming smaller, more regular meals during the day and ensuring you receive enough calories and nutrients.

4.2 Stage 4 CKD diet

Diet for a kidney disorder is based on other factors, such as diabetes. Chat regarding eating through your healthcare professional or inquire for a referral to a dietician.

A kidney disorder diet, in general, should be:

- Making fresh foods a preference over refined goods
- Have smaller meat, livestock, and fish portions,
- Require minimal to no alcohol intake
- Limit processed sugars, cholesterol, and saturated fats
- Salt elimination

The amounts of phosphorus may be too high or too poor, so it's necessary to go over the most recent blood work. High-phosphorus foods include:

- Dairy products
- Nut butter
- Beans, peas, and lentils that have been dried
- Bran
- Nuts
- Dark cola, chocolate, beer,

If the levels of potassium are too high, reduce:

- Melons, bananas, oranges, and dried fruit
- Avocados, tomatoes, and potatoes
- Vegetables with dark leaves
- Wild and brown rice
- Dairy Foods
- Beans, oats, as well as nuts
- Cereal bran, whole wheat pizza, spaghetti,
- Salt substitutes
- Meat, chicken, pork, and fish

At any visit with your healthcare professional, make sure to discuss your food. After evaluating the new exams, you can have to make changes. Speak to your healthcare professional regarding which nutritional medicines you can take, if any, and if you should adjust your fluid consumption or not.

CHAPTER 5

Prevention

C KD (Chronic kidney disease) cannot often be avoided, although you should take measures to decrease the risk of developing the infection.

You will reduce the chance by following the guidelines below.

Manage the vital requirements

When you have had a long-term illness that could progress to CKD, like elevated blood pressure or diabetes, it's essential to be properly managed.

Respect your GP's recommendations, take every medication recommended for you, and hold all appointments about your illness.

Avoid smoking

It is proved that smoking increases coronary disease chances, including cardiac attacks or seizures, which are correlated with a greater risk of having CKD.

Discontinuing smoking will boost your physical wellbeing and decrease your chance of all these serious effects.

All recipes in this cookbook are renal friendly. This cookbook is designed for Stage 3 and Stage 4 Patients to satisfy their nutritional and caloric needs. This book is not recommended for the later stages of CKD patients. They should follow their dieticians and physicians' guidelines strictly.

CHAPTER 6

Sauces and Seasonings

This section is a treasure for kidney patients because all these seasonings and sauces are low sodium and tailored according to kidney patients' needs. All recipes can be made ahead and stored for up to 3 months. Easily used for marinades and as dips for bread, tortillas, and chips, also best for dressings and flavorful sodium-free spice blends that work well with meat dishes and sauces.

1. 60-Second Salsa

Ingredients

- Tomatoes, Roma or plum, 4 chopped
- Onions, green, 2 chopped
- Garlic cloves, 3, minced
- Bell pepper, green, ½ cup, chopped
- Fresh jalapeño, ½ - 1, ½ bunch chopped
- Fresh cilantro, chopped
- Cumin, ½ tsp
- Fresh oregano, ¼ cup, chopped (or dried, 1 tbsp)

Directions

1. Combine all ingredients with a food processor or blend in a blender till the big items are chunky and small in size.
2. Refrigerator for a few hours.
3. Serve chilled along with plain tortilla chips.

2. Apple & Cherry Chutney

Ingredients

- Tart apple, 1 medium
- Tart cherries, dried, 1 cup
- Red onion, 1 small, thinly sliced
- Apple cider vinegar, 1 cup
- Sugar, 1 ½ cups

Directions

1. Core and quarter the apple, then cut with the skin on into thin slices.
2. In a heavy saucepan, put the cherries and apples with the onions, sugar, and vinegar. Cook and keep stirring till the sugar is dissolved and starts to boil.
3. Reduce flame to low. Cover and cook until the onions are soft and the dried cherries are soft and plump, for about 8 to 10 minutes.
4. Uncover and increase the flame to high and boil until the fruit's syrup has reduced to a glossy glaze. It will take about 5 minutes more. This Chutney can be served at once or kept in the fridge for several days.

3. Basil Oil

Ingredients

- Fresh basil leaves, 1 ½ cups
- Vegetable oil or olive oil, 1 cup

Directions

1. Wash and drain the basil leaves.
2. Pat dry with a paper towel.
3. Combine vegetable oil or olive oil with the basil leaves in a food processor or a blender. Blitz just till leaves are finely chopped (do not puree).
4. Transfer mixture into a large pan on medium heat. Mix occasionally till oil bubbles the sides and temperature state 165 degrees on a food thermometer, about three to4 minutes. The oil must be heated to eliminate any bacteria in the oil mixture.
5. Take off from heat and put aside to cool for about an hour.
6. Fix two layers of cheesecloth on a fine wire strainer and arrange it on a small bowl.
7. Transfer oil mixture into the strainer.
8. When oil passes through, press gently on the basil to release the remaining oil.
9. Throw away basil.
10. Serve oil with a salad or use it as a dip for bread.
11. It may be stored in an airtight container for up to 3 months in the refrigerator.

4. BBQ Rub for Pork or Chicken

Ingredients

- Brown sugar, 1 tbsp
- Allspice, ⅛ tsp
- Smoked paprika, 1 tsp
- Ground red pepper ⅛ tsp (optional)
- Chili powder, 1 tsp
- Garlic, granulated, 1 tsp
- Dry mustard powder, ¼ tsp
- Onion powder, 1 tsp
- Cumin, 1 tsp

Directions

1. Blend all Ingredients In a bowl together thoroughly.
2. Marinate chicken or pork with this seasoning before cooking.

5. Cajun Seasoning

Ingredients

- Paprika, 2 tsp
- Onion powder, 2 tsp
- Garlic powder, 2 tsp
- Cayenne, 1 tsp for mild or 2 tsp for medium spice

Directions

1. Combine all ingredients and stock in an airtight jar.

6. Buttermilk Herb Ranch Dressing

Ingredients

- Mayonnaise, ½ cup
- Milk, ½ cup
- Vinegar, 2 tbsp
- Fresh chives, 1 tbsp chopped
- Dill, 1 tbsp
- Oregano leaves, 1 tbsp, chopped
- Garlic powder, ¼ tsp

Directions

1. Whisk mayonnaise, vinegar, and milk in a medium mixing bowl.
2. Then add fresh dill, oregano leaves, chives, and garlic powder.
3. Blend together.
4. For one hour, chill to allow flavors to develop.
5. Before serving, mix the dressing well.

7. Chinese Five-Spice Blend

Ingredients

- Ginger, ¼ cup
- Ground cinnamon, 2 tbsp
- Anise seed, 1 tsp
- Ground cloves, 2 tsp
- Ground allspice, 1 tsp

Directions

1. Combine all ingredients together and keep in an airtight jar.
2. Ground spices stay fresh for one year

8. Citrus Relish

Ingredients

- Limes, kumquats, small lemons, or oranges, 2 pounds
- White vinegar, 1 quart
- Mustard seed, ¼ cup
- Glass jars
- Sugar, 2-4 tbsp

Directions

For Pickled Fruit
1. Cut each fruit with a cross at the stem. Quarter oranges, if using.
2. Fill glass jars with cut fruit and pour in vinegar.
3. To each jar, add in 2 tsp of mustard seed. Screw on lids.
4. About one month, keep it at room temperature, then make it into relish as below.

For Citrus Relish
5. Mix the fruit with sugar in a small saucepan, and add more sugar if required.
6. Stir the pan often on medium heat till the mixture boils, and the fruits turn glossy and translucent, for about 5-10 minutes.
7. Serve cool or warm.
8. The vinegar leftover from the pickled fruit may be used to marinate fish or poultry or in salad dressings

9. Creamy Basil Vinaigrette Dressing

Ingredients

- Olive oil, ½ cup
- Red wine vinegar, ¼ cup
- Fresh basil, 1 tbsp
- Granulated sugar, 2 tsp
- Ground pepper, ¼ tsp
- Garlic, 1 clove pressed

Directions

1. Puree all ingredients together in a blender until smooth.

10. Fajita Marinade

Ingredients

- Limes, juiced, 2
- Orange, juiced, 1
- Grapefruit, juiced, 1
- Jalapeño, finely diced, 1
- Garlic, 2 cloves crushed or dried, ¼ tsp
- Vegetable oil

Directions

1. Combine every ingredient in a small container.
2. Pour on vegetables and meat to coat.
3. Marinate for at least two hours before grilling, pan-frying, or barbequing.

11. Dilled Cream Cheese Spread

Ingredients

- Whipped cream cheese, 8 oz
- Onion powder, 1 tsp
- Fresh dill, ½ tsp, chopped

Directions

1. With an electric mixer, mix all ingredients together,
2. Keep in an airtight jar in the refrigerator.

12. Fruit & Herb Vinegars

Ingredients

- Vinegar, such as white, cider, white or red wine, 1-quart bottle
- Fruit or berries, ½ cup, your choice, cut into half-inch pieces
- Fresh herbs, your choice, 3-4 sprigs
- Salad dressing jars or bottles

Directions

1. Take out ½ a cup of vinegar from the bottle.
2. Wash and cut fruit. Chop pieces about ½ inch. Put fruits into the vinegar bottle. For small fruits like blackberries or blueberries, just drop them in the bottle.
3. Cap the bottle and keep it at room temperature for about one month.
4. Filter vinegar through a jelly bag, cheesecloth, or strainer.
5. Transfer into jars, adding a few fresh fruits or a new sprig of herbs!
6. Store at room temperature or refrigerate, last up to one year.

Different Combinations

Kiwi /Lemon Grass/Mandarin Orange,
Tarragon and Italian Plum
Blackberry and vanilla bean
For savory kinds of vinegar: basil, garlic, and tomato, or sage, leek, and thyme.
Always keep the volume per quart of vinegar to about ½ cup of fruit and herbs.

13. Healthy Low Sodium Gravy

Ingredients

- Water, 10 cups
- Turkey neck or giblets, 250 g
- Onion, 1 cup, chopped
- Garlic, 1 tbsp, minced
- Carrots, 1 cup, chopped
- Celery, 1 cup, chopped
- Olive oil, 2 tbsp
- Fresh parsley, ½ cup, chopped
- Fresh marjoram or thyme, 2 tbsp (stems removed)
- Flour, ½ cup
- Unsalted butter, 1 cup
- Cider vinegar, 2 tbsp

Directions

1. Add water, turkey bits, sliced vegetables, garlic, and herbs to a big pot to prepare a broth.
2. Take it to a boil and cook for 1 hour or so.
3. Toast the flour in the oven on a baking sheet till lightly brown at 350 degrees, mixing once or twice for around 10 minutes.
4. In a saucepan, heat the butter. Over medium heat, whisk the flour into the heated butter.
5. Strain the broth with a fine sieve.
6. Take the meat out of the neck, cut the giblets, and place it back in the broth.
7. Adding 3 cups of broth to the mixture of butter/flour and boil on medium heat. Stirring the mixture until it's thick.
8. Return to a large pot with the remaining broth.
9. Get the stock to a simmer, sometimes stirring, over high heat.
10. Lower the heat and simmer for 5-10 minutes, stirring regularly.
11. Only before eating incorporate apple vinegar.

14. Homemade Low-Sodium Soy Sauce

Ingredients

- Sodium Free Bouillon, 5 packets, chicken flavor
- Balsamic vinegar, 6 tbsp
- Molasses, 4-5 tbsp
- Boiling water, 2 cups
- Black pepper, ¼ tsp
- Powdered ginger, ¼ tsp
- Garlic powder, ¼ tsp
- Kikkoman Soy Sauce, Less Sodium, 2 tbsp

Directions

1. Mix up all the ingredients.
2. Transfer into the bottle and keep it in the refrigerator. Keeps indefinitely.

15. HONEY LEMON DRESSING

INGREDIENTS

- Worcestershire sauce, ¼ cup
- Brown sugar, ¾ cup
- Soy sauce, low sodium, ¼ cup
- Ketchup, no-salt-added, ¾ cup
- Rice wine (or other white) vinegar, ¼ cup
- Canola oil, 2 tbsp

- Mustard, 2 tbsp
- Garlic powder, ½ tsp
- Black pepper, ground, ⅛ tsp
- Onion powder, ½ tsp

DIRECTIONS

1. With a whisk, blend all the ingredients well.
2. Use up immediately or keep in the refrigerator.

17. LIME GINGER SAUCE

INGREDIENTS

- White grape juice, 1 cup
- Lime juice, fresh, ¼ cup
- White wine vinegar, ⅓ cup
- Fresh ginger, 1 tbsp, minced
- Fresh garlic, 1 tbsp, minced
- Heavy cream, ½ cup
- Butter, 1 ½ stick, cold unsalted, cut into chunks

- Thai sweet chili sauce, ¼ cup
- Pepper, ¼ tsp

DIRECTIONS

1. Combine grape juice, vinegar, lime juice, ginger, and garlic in a large saucepan on medium heat.
2. Put to a boil; minimize to a soft syrup by 90%.
3. Add in cream and decrease by 60%, stirring slowly so as not to burn the sauce.
4. Lower the heat to a minimum and stir in bits of cold butter steadily.
5. Stir the chili sauce in it.
6. Sprinkle with pepper.
7. Keep warm till ready to serve.

18. Low Salt Ketchup

Ingredients

- Onion, ¾ cup, chopped
- Cider vinegar, ½ cup
- Sugar, ⅓ cup
- Molasses, 1 tbsp
- Dry mustard, 2 tsp
- Celery seed, ½ tsp
- Ground cinnamon, ¼ tsp
- Cloves, ¼ tsp
- Dried basil, ¼ tsp
- Dried tarragon, ¼ tsp
- Pepper, ¼ tsp
- Garlic, 1 clove minced
- Water, 1 cup
- Tomato paste, 2 (6-oz.) can

Directions

1. In a blender or food processor, put all ingredients, excluding tomato paste and water, and blend till smooth.
2. Transfer the mixture to a large saucepan or a Dutch oven.
3. Add 3 cups of water and two 6-oz Cans of tomato paste.
4. Heat on low, uncovered, for around 35 minutes or till the mixture has decreased to half the original volume, stirring periodically.
5. Pour in the jars and keep in the fridge for up to 1 month. Or freeze up to 10 months.

19. Low Salt Dijon-style Mustard

Ingredients

- Dry white wine, 1 cup
- Vinegar, ½ cup
- Onion, ¼ cup, chopped
- Sugar, 1 tbsp
- Dried tarragon, ½ tsp, crushed
- Allspice, 5 wholes
- Garlic, 2 cloves minced
- Bay leaf, 1
- Red pepper, ¼ tsp, ground

Directions

1. In a 1000ml saucepan, mix all the ingredients.
2. Boil uncovered for around 20 minutes on medium-high heat or until the liquid is decreased by half.
3. Meanwhile, stir ¼ cup cold water and ½ cup dry mustard together in a bowl; put aside for 10 minutes.
4. Strain the mixture of vinegar into the mustard mix, press out all the liquid, and remove the solids.
5. Stir in the mixture; return to the pan.
6. Cook uncovered for around 10 minutes on medium-low heat or till heavy cream is consistent, stirring regularly.
7. Set aside to cool down, Cover and refrigerate.
8. Up to 2 months of storage in the refrigerator.

20. Mexican Blend

Ingredients

- Chili powder, ¼ cup
- Ground cumin, 1 tbsp
- Dried oregano, 1 tsp
- Onion powder, 1 tbsp
- Garlic powder, 1 tsp
- Cinnamon, ½ tsp
- Crushed red pepper, 1 tsp

Directions

1. Combine all ingredients and keep them in an airtight jar.

21. Microwave Berry Jam

Ingredients

- Mashed berries, 1 cup (any kind or combination)
- Granulated sugar, ¾ cup
- Unsalted butter, ¼ tsp
- Lemon juice, 1 tsp

Directions

1. Place all ingredients in a microwave-proof bowl and stir.
2. For 5 minutes, microwave on high for all berries, excluding strawberries. They should be microwaved for 4 minutes.
3. Mix.
4. Microwave for another 5 minutes (4 for Strawberries).
5. Put in a jar with a lid or cover with a plastic wrap, keep refrigerated.
6. It can be kept for several months.

22. Mixed Herb Blend

Ingredients

- Dried oregano, 1 tbsp
- Dried parsley, ¼ cup
- Celery seed, 1 tbsp
- Dried tarragon, 2 tbsp
- Dill weed, 1 tbsp

Directions

1. Combine all ingredients and keep them in an airtight jar.

23. Simple White Sauce

Ingredients

- Flour, 2 tbsp
- Unsalted butter, 2 tbsp
- Heavy cream, 1 cup
- Dry mustard, ¼ tsp
- Paprika, ¼ tsp
- Basil, parsley, or other herbs, 1 tsp dried or ½ tsp fresh

Directions

1. In a measuring cup of 2 cup glass or a little microwave-safe tub, mix flour and butter together.
2. 30 seconds in the microwave, stir, another 30 seconds in the microwave.
3. Include the spices and cream and stir.
4. Microwave for 1 minute. Again, stir.
5. 1 minute in the microwave.
6. Add 1 more minute if it has not thickened.

24. Savory Seasoning

Ingredients

- Celery seed, 1 ¼ tsp
- Marjoram, 2 tbsp, crushed or ground
- Sage, 2 tbsp, crushed or ground
- Thyme, 2 tbsp, crushed or ground
- Basil, 1 tbsp, crushed or ground

Directions

1. Mix all ingredients well and keep in a salt shaker or spice jar.

25. Spicy Thai Marinade

Ingredients

- Soy sauce, reduced-sodium, ¼ cup
- Asian oyster sauce, 2 tbsp
- Minced garlic, 1 tbsp
- Fresh ginger, 1 tbsp, minced
- Red chili paste, ½ - 1 tsp
- Green onion, 2 tbsp minced
- Cilantro, 2 tbsp minced

Directions

1. Mix together the fish sauce, soy, sugar, garlic, ginger, and chili paste in a large bowl or wide zip lock bag until well mixed.
2. Stir or turn regularly to brush chicken uniformly with marinade; transfer chicken, cover, or seal tightly and chill for at least 30 minutes or approximately for one day.
3. Drain and discard the chicken marinade.
4. To barbecue:
5. Sprinkle the chopped onion and cilantro on the fried chicken.

26. Savory Mushroom Sauce

Ingredients

- Butter, 2 tbsp
- Dry sherry, 2 tbsp
- Lime juice, 1 tbsp
- Minced dry onion, 1 tbsp
- Chives, parsley, and tarragon, 1 tsp each, finely chopped
- Garlic powder, ½ tsp

- Fresh mushrooms, 1 pound (about 5 ½ Cups) halved

Directions

1. Mix the butter, lime juice, sherry, garlic powder, and herbs in a 2-quart microwave-safe serving bowl.
2. Microwave uncovered for 1 minute on 100 percent strength (high), stirring once.
3. Stir the mushrooms in.
4. Microwave for 6 to 8 minutes or till soft, stirring twice.

27. Poultry Seasoning

Ingredients

- Dried ground sage, 2 tbsp
- Dried thyme, 2 tsp
- Ground black pepper, 1 tsp
- Dried marjoram, 2 tsp

Directions

1. Combine all ingredients together in a small bowl.
2. Add to a spice jar or other airtight container.

28. Middle Eastern Seasoning

Ingredients

- Ground coriander, 1 tsp
- Ground cumin, 1 tsp
- Turmeric powder, 1 tbsp
- Ground cloves, ¼ tsp
- Paprika, 1 tsp
- Cayenne pepper, ¼ tsp

Directions

1. Combine ingredients well and keep them in a salt shaker or spice jar.

29. Giblet Gravy

Ingredients

- Egg, chopped & boiled, 1
- All-purpose flour, 1 tbsp.
- Poultry liver/giblets, chopped, 1 or 2
- Chicken broth, 2 cups

Directions

1. With a whisk, mix flour to 1 tbsp of broth till smooth.
2. Add in the remaining broth and simmer on low heat, continuously stirring.
3. Giblets and boiled egg to be included.
4. Keep stirring till the desired thickness (about five minutes).

CHAPTER 7

Breakfast

All our recipes are low in sodium, potassium, and phosphorus. Patients who are advised to take low protein should limit their intake of dairy products. They may not eliminate dairy products from their food, but instead, limiting their portion sizes will also help lower protein levels and maintain their nutrition and caloric intake.

30. Renal-friendly French Toast

Ingredients

- egg whites, 4 large, slightly beaten
- white bread, 4 slices (maybe toasted)
- 1% milk, ¼ cup
- margarine, 1 tbsp
- cinnamon, ½ tsp
- allspice, ¼ tsp

Directions

1. Beat egg whites, adding milk, allspice, and cinnamon.
2. One slice at a time, soak bread into the egg mix.
3. Heat a skillet and melt margarine Place a slice of soaked bread on the skillet.
4. Fry each side of bread till golden brown.
5. Drizzle with syrup and serve hot (sugar-free if diabetic).

31. Creamy Porridge

Ingredients

- milk, 70 ml
- porridge oats, 1 oz
- water, 70 ml

Directions

1. Stove method
2. In a saucepan, place the oats; add the water and milk in and blend.
3. Take to a boil and cook for 4-5 minutes, mixing from time to time and closely watching that the pan's bottom does not stick.
4. Whisk the porridge as it is cooking for a fluffier porridge.
5. Put aside and serve after 30 to 60 seconds,
6. For flavor, sugar, pasteurized honey, or artificial sweetener can be added.
7. Microwave method
8. In a big microwaveable cup, blend the oats with milk and water.
9. Microwave on full for 3 minutes, halfway around, stirring or whisking.
10. Until eating, leave it to rest for 2 minutes.
11. For flavor, sugar, pasteurized honey, or artificial sweetener can be added.

32. BANANA CHOCOLATE CHIP MUFFINS

INGREDIENTS

- Over-ripe bananas, 2 larges, mashed
- Plain yogurt, 2 tbsp
- Light brown sugar, ⅓ cup
- All-purpose flour, unbleached, 1 cup
- Large egg, 1
- Olive oil, ¼ cup
- Dark chocolate chips, ⅔ cup
- Baking soda, ½ tsp
- Nutmeg, ¼ tsp
- Almonds, ⅓ cup sliced
- Vanilla extract, 1 tsp
- Sea salt, ¼ tsp

DIRECTIONS

1. Heat the oven to 350°F.
2. Brush muffin molds with oil or fill with muffin liners.
3. Mix together bananas, egg, oil, and sugar in a medium-sized mixing bowl and stir well.
4. Include vanilla and yogurt and mix with a spatula until smooth.
5. Add in the flour ¼ cup at a time, adding baking soda and salt in between additions.
6. Mix all thoroughly.
7. Sprinkle chocolate chips and almonds.
8. Bake for 12 minutes approximately. Serve and enjoy.

33. OVERNIGHT OATS

INGREDIENTS

- Rolled oats, 1 ½ cups
- Coconut milk, canned, 1 cup
- Almond milk, unsweetened, 1 ½ cups
- Chia seeds, 2 tbsp
- Ground cinnamon, ½ tsp (Optional)

DIRECTIONS

1. Place all ingredients in a glass jar or bowl and mix to combine.
2. Cover or seal and keep in the fridge for around 8 hours or overnight.
3. Split in serving bowls and garnish with the desired toppings (almonds, seeds, coconut flakes, berries)

34. Cherry Tomato and Basil Omelets

Ingredients

- Small eggs, 2
- Olive oil, 1 tbsp
- Cherry tomatoes, 3
- Fresh black pepper, ¼ tsp
- Fresh basil, 1 tbsp

Directions

1. In a mixing cup, break the eggs.
2. Add black pepper, freshly ground.
3. Using a fork to beat well
4. Slice the cherry tomatoes in two and add the olive oil to the small frying pan over a high flame.
5. For around 1 minute, fry the tomatoes, then reduce the heat down a bit.
6. Adding the eggs, then rotate the pan around to distribute them out uniformly.
7. When the omelet starts to cook and firm and has a bit of raw egg on top, scatter over the fresh basil leaves.
8. Using a spatula, ease along the side of the omelet.
9. Remove the frying pan from the fire and slip the omelet onto a serving plate as it continues to turn light golden beneath.

35. French Toast

Ingredients

- egg, 1 medium-sized
- butter, 1 tsp
- milk, 50 ml, low fat
- maple syrup, 1 tbsp
- bread, 1 thick slice

Directions

1. Whisk the milk and egg together.
2. Dip the bread into the egg mix.
3. Heat butter in a heavy frying pan on medium heat.
4. Adding soaked bread to the hot pan, fry for 2 to 3 minutes on each side.
5. drizzle with maple syrup
6. serve

36. Peanut Butter and Jelly Oats

Ingredients

- Rolled oats, 1 ½ cups
- Coconut milk, canned, 1 cup
- Almond milk, unsweetened, 1 ½ cups
- Chia seeds, 2 Tbsp.
- For topping
- Fresh or frozen berries, pureed
- Peanut butter

Directions

1. Place all ingredients in a glass jar or bowl and mix to combine.
2. Cover or seal and keep in the fridge for around 8 hours or overnight.
3. Mix in ½ cup pureed berries and 4 tbsp peanut butter
4. Split in serving bowls and serve.

37. Simple Pancakes

Ingredients

- All-purpose flour, ½ cup
- 2% milk, ¼ cup, plus ¼ cup water
- Granulated sugar, ¼ cup
- Vegetable oil, 1 tbsp
- Egg, 1, beaten
- baking powder, ¼ tsp

Directions

1. Mix the flour, egg, sugar, baking powder in a bowl. Thoroughly blend. Put in some milk. For pancakes, substitute water for a thinner batter or fewer for thicker pancakes.
2. Heat the oil in a pan. Put ¼ cup of flour batter into the pan at a time.
3. Make each side fried until golden.

38. Mexican Skillet Breakfast

Ingredients

- Beaten eggs, 8
- Green onions, 2, sliced thin, with greens
- Chili powder, 1 tsp
- Ketchup, low salt, ¼ cup
- Butter, 2 tbsp
- Unsalted tortilla chips, 1 bag (6 oz), broken up

Directions

1. Beat the eggs till they are fluffy.
2. Include chili powder, onion and ketchup. Beat until all ingredients are well combined again. Put aside.
3. In a frying pan, heat the butter, add in tortilla chips & sauté till cooked over medium heat. Pour in the whisked eggs & scramble till you get a perfect consistency. Serve immediately on hot plates.

39. Higher Protein Overnight Oats

Ingredients

- Rolled oats, 1 ½ cups
- Coconut milk, canned, 1 cup
- Soya milk, 1 ½ cups
- Chia seeds, 2 tbsp.

For topping
- Nut butter (any nut/seed butter)
- Ground cinnamon, ½ tsp (Optional)

Directions

1. Place all Ingredients in a glass jar or bowl and mix to combine.
2. Cover or seal and keep in the fridge for around 8 hours or overnight.
3. Split in serving bowls and put on toppings of 1 tbsp nut butter in each bowl.

40. Scrambled Egg

Ingredients

- Garlic bread, 1 slice
- Eggs, 2 smalls
- Olive oil, 1 tbsp
- Black pepper, ¼ tsp, freshly ground

Directions

1. Blend the eggs and fresh ground black pepper together gently.
2. Apply the oil and allow it to heat in a nonstick skillet. Pour the egg mixture in and let it stay for 20 seconds without stirring. Using a wooden spoon to stir, pick and fold it from the bottom of the skillet. Let it stay, then stir and fold once after another 10 seconds.
3. Repeat the process until the eggs are gently set and somewhat runny, then take off the heat and leave to cook for a few seconds. Giving the velvety scramble a final stir. Immediately serve.

41. Sweet Corn Pudding

Ingredients

- Kernel corn, 2 cups fresh cut or canned
- 1% milk, ½ cup
- Egg substitute, ¾ cup
- Onion, ⅓ cup, finely chopped
- Butter, 1 tbsp, melted
- Water, ½ cup
- Black pepper or white, 1 tsp
- Granulated sugar, 2 tsp

Directions

1. Heat the oven to 350°f.
2. Mix all items in a container.
3. Take a big casserole dish, oil it, and pour the mixed batter in it.
4. Put the casserole dish in a shallow pan filled with one inch of hot water.
5. Bake till middle sets or a knife inserted in the middle comes out clean or for about 40 to 45 minutes.
6. Let it rest at room temperature for about 10 minutes before serving.

42. Baked Fruit Oatmeal

Ingredients

- Oats, 2 ¼ cups (old fashioned, uncooked)
- Brown sugar, firmly packed, ⅓ cup (can substitute an artificial sweetener if desired)
- Salt, ¼ tsp (optional)
- Rice dream, original, 3 cups
- Eggs, lightly beaten, 3
- Butter, melted, 1 tbsp
- Vanilla, 1 tsp
- Almond extract, ¼ – ½ tsp
- Blueberries, frozen or fresh, ¾ cup

Directions

1. Heat oven up to 350° F. Spray eight ramekins or custard cups with cooking spray. Assemble on a rimmed baking tray.
2. In a large bowl, mix brown sugar, oats, and salt. Stir well.
3. In a medium bowl, blend together eggs, rice dream, butter, almond, and vanilla extract.
4. Combine both dry and wet ingredients. Combine well until blended. Scoop into cups. Put berries into every cup, dividing evenly.
5. Bake for about 25 to 30 minutes. (Middles will not be fully set.). Cool for 10 minutes.
6. Enjoy!

43. Pumpkin Pie Overnight Oats

Ingredients

- Rolled oats, 1 ½ cups
- Pumpkin puree, 2 tsp
- Almond milk, 1 ½ cups
- Chia seeds, 2 tbsp.

For topping
- Pumpkin pie spice blend
- Pecan sliced

Directions

1. Place all ingredients in a glass jar or bowl and mix to combine.
2. Cover or seal and keep in the fridge for around 8 hours or overnight.
3. Split in serving bowls, add toppings to your taste, and serve.

44. Kale and Cheddar Frittata

Ingredients

- Sharp cheddar cheese, 1 oz, shredded (or any sharp cheese)
- Eggs beaters, 8
- Lacinato kale, 4 oz (½ bunch), cut into ribbons
- Olive oil, 2 tbsps.
- Kosher salt, ¼ tsp
- Ground black pepper, ¼ tsp
- Red pepper flakes, ¼ tsp crushed
- Garlic, 2 cloves, minced

Directions

1. Heat oven to 350°F.
2. Prepare the eggs in a small bowl and put aside.
3. In an oven-safe skillet, heat the oil on medium heat. Add the kale, black pepper, salt, and red pepper and heat, occasionally stirring, until the kale starts to droop. Include the garlic and simmer for 2 more minutes. Take away from the heat.
4. Transfer the beaten eggs into the hot skillet and give it a quick mix with the kale. Scatter the cheese on top and roast in the oven till the eggs are set, for about 10 minutes. Portion into four equal wedges and serve.

45. Higher Calorie Overnight Oats

Ingredients

- Rolled oats, 1 ½ cups
- Coconut milk, canned, 1 cup
- Almond milk, 1 ½ cups
- Chia seeds, 2 tbsp.
- Ground cinnamon, ½ tsp (optional)

For topping
- Almonds sliced
- Seeds (pumpkin and sunflower)

Directions

1. Place all ingredients in a glass jar or bowl and mix to combine.
2. Cover or seal and keep in the fridge for around 8 hours or overnight.
3. Split in serving bowls, add toppings, and serve.

46. Spanish Tortilla

Ingredients

- Potatoes, golden, 5 smalls
- beaten eggs, 8
- onion, 1 large, halved and sliced
- red bell pepper, 1 small, diced
- olive oil, 1 cup, (½ cup will be left and reused)
- black pepper, ¼ tsp, ground
- salt, ¼ tsp

Directions

1. Preheat oven to 400°F.
2. Split the potatoes halfway across. Put the flat surface of each half of it on the chopping board and cut it thinly.
3. Prepare potatoes according to lo potassium potatoes recipe given in recipes.
4. Heat olive oil over low heat in a low nonstick skillet that is ovenproof.
5. Include bell pepper and onion and fry for five minutes. Include the prepared potato slices and sauté until the potatoes are lightly browned around 7-8 minutes.
6. Include black pepper over the vegetables and swirl to combine. Drain the extra cooking oil from the pan and transfer it into a container. Cooldown the vegetables marginally.
7. In a big mixing dish, beat the egg beaters and salt.
8. Shift the strained cooked vegetables into the beaten egg.
9. Transfer 1 tbsp of the remaining oil to the pan and cook over medium flame.
10. Place the mix of veggies and eggs into the heated skillet. Mix with the spoon and allow the egg to thicken a little bit for 3-5 minutes.
11. Lower the heat and cook for another 10 minutes. Shake the skillet softly with its handle for a minute or two to ensure the bottom does not stick.
12. Move the skillet to the oven while the top is also a little undercooked, yet you can tell the bottom is strong. Bake until the top is cooked for 7-8 minutes.
13. Serve instantly with a salad or set aside for later meals

47. Apple and Zucchini Harvest Muffins

Ingredients

- Whole wheat pastry flour, 1 cup (or all-purpose flour if unavailable)
- All-purpose flour, ½ cup
- Baking powder, one tsp
- Baking soda, ½ tsp
- Ground flax seeds, ¼ cup
- Ground cinnamon, 1 tsp
- Canola oil, ⅓ cup
- Sugar, ¼ cup
- Apple cider vinegar, 1 tbsp
- Egg, 1
- Unsweetened applesauce, ½ cup
- Sugar, ¼ cup
- Molasses, 1 tbsp
- Sugar, ¼ cup

Directions

1. Heat oven to 425°F.
2. Prepare a muffin tray with nonstick spray for baking. In a big bowl, mix the flour, cinnamon, baking soda, flax seeds, baking powder together.
3. Blend the oil, apple cider vinegar, sugar, egg, molasses, and applesauce together in another container until well mixed. Mix in the apples and the zucchini.
4. Put dry ingredients together and add the wet ingredients. Stir to mix a few times. To the prepared muffin cups, add batter.
5. Cook at 425 ° F for 5 minutes and then reduce the oven temperature to 350 ° F.
6. Serve warm.

48. BAGEL BREAD PUDDING

INGREDIENTS

- Cooking spray
- Bagels, 2 medium-sized
- Milk, 1 cup
- Egg product, low cholesterol in liquid form, ½ cup
- Sugar, ½ cup
- Cinnamon, 1 tsp

DIRECTIONS

1. Spray a 1 ½quart (3 cups) baking dish with cooking spray.
2. Break the bagels into little pieces and put them in a baking dish.
3. Blend together the egg product, milk, cinnamon, and sugar.
4. Spread over bagel pieces, then put aside for 2 minutes till the bagels soak in the liquid.
5. Bake in a 350 F oven until browned on top for about 30 minutes.
6. Serve cold or warm.

49. BERRY OATMEAL MUFFINS

INGREDIENTS

- All-purpose flour, unbleached, 1 cup
- Oatmeal, quick-cooking, ½ cup
- Brown sugar, lightly packed, ⅔ cup
- Baking soda, ½ tsp
- Eggs, 2
- Canola oil, ¼ cup
- Raspberries, fresh or frozen, ¾ cup
- Blueberries, fresh or frozen, ¾ cup
- Applesauce, ½ cup
- Zest of 1 orange
- Zest of 1 lemon
- Lemon juice, 1 tbsp

DIRECTIONS

1. Heat the oven to 350 °F/180 °C. Line a 12muffin tin with silicone liners or paper.
2. In a mixing bowl, mix the flour, brown sugar, oatmeal, and baking soda. Put aside.
3. In another large bowl, blend the eggs, oil, applesauce, lemon juice, and citrus zest. Mix in all the dry ingredients with a wooden spoon. Add in the berries & stir gently.
4. Spoon batter into the lined muffin cups. Put in the oven for 20- 22 minutes or till a toothpick put in the middle of a muffin emerges clean. Let cool.

50. Chocolate Overnight Oats

Ingredients

- Rolled oats, 1 ½ cups
- Coconut milk, canned, 1 cup
- Almond milk, 1 ½ cups
- Chia seeds, 2 tbsp.
- Cocoa powder, ¼ cup
- For topping
- Almonds sliced

Directions

1. Place all ingredients in a glass jar or bowl and mix to combine.
2. Cover or seal and keep in the fridge for around 8 hours or overnight.
3. Split in serving bowls, add toppings, and serve.

51. Cranberry Nut Bread

Ingredients

- Cranberries dried, 1 ½ cups
- All-purpose flour, 2 cups
- Sugar, 1 cup
- Baking powder, 1 ½ tsp
- Baking soda, ½ tsp
- Apple juice, ½ cup
- Orange zest, 1 tsp
- Margarine, melted, 2 tbsp
- Egg, 1, lightly beaten
- Walnuts, chopped, ¼ cup
- Hot water, 2 tbsp

Directions

1. Slice all cranberries in half and set them aside
2. Heat oven to 350 F.
3. Oil a loaf pan and apply with waxed paper.
4. Combine sugar, flour, baking soda, and baking powder together and sift into a large mixing bowl.
5. In another bowl, mix melted margarine, apple juice, beaten egg, and orange zest.
6. Add wet mixture to the flour mixture and mix until flour is well combined.
7. Add in walnuts and cranberries.
8. Mix in the heated water.
9. Pour batter in greased and lined loaf pan and place in the heated oven for 1 hour and 10 minutes.
10. Examine by pricking a toothpick into the bread; if it comes out neat, the bread is done.
11. Take out from the pan and let rest on a wire rack for 2 minutes. Serve.

52. Egg Salad with easy Biscuit

Ingredients

- Mayonnaise Ingredients: (makes 1 cup, can be stored for up to 10 days)
- Medium egg, 1
- Lemon juice, 2 tsp, freshly squeezed
- Sunflower, 1 cup (or other vegetable oil)
- Biscuit Ingredients: (makes 6)
- All-purpose flour, 1 cup
- Baking powder, 1 ½ tsp
- Sugar, 1 tbsp
- Cold butter, ¼ cup (chilled in the freezer for 20 min)
- Whole milk, ⅓ cup
- Large egg, 1

- Egg Salad Ingredient:
- Homemade Mayonnaise, ¼ cup
- Medium eggs, 4
- Celery, ¾ cup, diced
- Red onion, ¼ cup
- Carrots, ¼ cup, grated
- Cornichon pickles, 4
- Dijon mustard, 1 tsp
- Black pepper, ¼ tsp, freshly ground
- Fresh parsley, 1 tbsp, chopped
- Fresh dill, 1 tbsp, chopped

Directions

For Mayonnaise:
1. Into the blender, break an egg.
2. If using, include the salt and lemon juice.
3. Pour a continual stream of sunflower oil into the blender at the medium level.
4. Raise the speed as the mixture thickens.
5. After pouring the oil, keep blending a bit. Put it aside, set it back.

For Biscuit:
6. Heat the oven to 425 ° F and line with parchment paper, a baking sheet.
7. In a big mixing bowl, mix the flour, sugar, salt, and baking powder. Mix thoroughly. Put aside.
8. Rub the butter into the flour, using your fingertips or a pastry cutter only until the mixture imitates coarse crumbs.
9. Include the egg and milk. Stir until they're all mixed well.
10. Move the biscuit dough to a well-floured table. Lightly knead. If it becomes too sticky, incorporate the flour till it's manageable.
11. Using both hands to stretch the dough till the mixture is an inch thick. Straight down the pastry, push a biscuit cutter, and transfer the Biscuit to the prepared baking tray.
12. Repeat until you've got about six biscuits, ½ inch away on the baking tray.
13. Bake for around 12 minutes or till the top is golden brown.

For Egg Salad:
14. Full boil eggs.
15. For 2 minutes, immerse boiled eggs in cold water.
16. Peel and chop them. Put in a medium bowl.
17. Include sliced celery, onion, pickles, and carrots.
18. Adding ¼ cup Dijon mustard, homemade mayo, salt, herbs, and pepper (if using). Mix thoroughly.
19. Serve cut in half on a warm biscuit.

53. Overnight High-Calorie Oats

Ingredients

- Rolled oats, ½ cups
- Almonds, coconut flakes, 3 tbsp
- Chia seeds, 2 tbsp.
- Coconut milk, canned, 1 cup
- Almond milk, unsweetened, ½ cups
- Ground cinnamon, ½ tsp (optional)

Directions

1. Place all Ingredients except almonds and coconut flakes in a glass jar or bowl and mix to combine.
2. Cover or seal and keep in the fridge for around 8 hours or overnight.
3. Split in serving bowls and garnish with remainder almonds, seeds, coconut flakes, berries

54. Renal Diet Breakfast: Loaded Veggie Eggs

Ingredients

- Whole eggs, 4
- Cauliflower, 1 cup
- Fresh spinach, 3 cups
- Garlic, 1 clove, minced
- Bell pepper, ¼ cup, chopped
- Onion, ¼ cup, chopped
- Black pepper, ¼ tsp
- Oil of choice, 1 tbsp (avocado oil or coconut oil is best for high heat)
- For garnish
- Spring onion and fresh parsley

Directions

1. Beat the eggs with the pepper until they are light and fluffy, put aside.
2. Heat oil in a broad skillet over medium heat.
3. Add the peppers and onions to the skillet and sauté till the onions are golden and translucent.
4. Add garlic, mix quickly to blend, and immediately incorporate cauliflower and spinach.
5. Fry the vegetables, turn the heat to medium-low and cook covered for 5 minutes.
6. Put in the eggs, whisk to mix with the vegetables.
7. When cooked thoroughly, garnish with spring onions or fresh parsley. Serves 2

CHAPTER 8

Salads

55. Chicken Salad with Yoghurt & Mint Dressing

Ingredients

- Chicken breasts, skinless, 2
- Celery, 1 stick
- Pineapple rings, drained & chopped, 2 cans
- Grapes, seedless, sliced in half, 5
- Mint yogurt dressing

- Mayonnaise low fat, 1 ½ tbsp
- Natural yogurt, low fat, 5oz carton
- Lemon juice, ½ tsp
- White pepper, ¼ tsp
- Honey, 1 tsp
- Fresh mint finely chopped, 2 tsp

Directions

1. Put the chicken in boiling water and cook on low for 30 minutes or till the chicken is fully cooked.
2. Drain and bring to room temperature
3. Break the chicken into small pieces and put in a bowl adding the sliced celery, pineapple pieces, and grapes.
4. To prepare the mint yogurt dressing, place all ingredients in a tub & blend to combine.
5. Add into the vegetable and chicken mixture, chill till ready to serve

56. Pineapple Carrot Salad

Ingredients

- Apricot nectar, 10 oz
- Gelatin, unflavored, 1 packet
- Sugar, ½ cup
- Cream cheese (low fat), 8 oz

- Whipping cream, 1 cup
- Pineapple, 8 oz can chop
- Carrots, 1 cup, shredded

Directions

1. To chill, bring a glass bowl & beaters from a hand blender into the freezer.
2. In a small saucepan, add 1 cup of apricot nectar and heat to a low boil. In a tub, put the gelatin and add the hot nectar into the gelatin & whisk to dissolve. Pour the remaining canned pineapple and nectar into the gelatin mixture, including liquid. Pour in the carrots. Put until partly set in the refrigerator.
3. Mix the cream cheese & sugar in a different cup. Set aside.
4. Take from the freezer chilled glass bowl, then add in the strong whipping cream. Pound to whip at high intensity for 3-4 minutes. Fold whipped cream softly into the mixture of cream cheese.
5. Over the partly set gelatin mixture, pour cream cheese mixture and combine softly. Refrigerate for approximately 3-4 hours.

57. Cran-Apple Salad

Ingredients

- Red apples, medium, 4
- Sugar, ¼ cup
- Cranberries, fresh, 2 cups
- Fruit-Fresh Produce Protector, 1 tbsp.
- Marshmallows (miniature), 1 cup

Directions

1. Core and peel apples. In a food processor, put cranberries and apples and chop.
2. Sprinkle and blend well with Fruit Fresh.
3. Fold in the butter and marshmallows.
4. Refrigerate for at least 4 hours.
5. Mix and serve.

58. Frosty Grapes

Ingredients

- Flavored gelatin, 3 oz
- Grapes (without seeds), 5 cups

Directions

1. Clean the grapes and de-steam them, making them mildly wet.
2. In a bowl, pour the dry mix of gelatin. Don't dissolve with water.
3. Put the wet grapes in the bowl & toss until evenly covered.
4. On a baking sheet, put the coated grapes on a single plate, or lay the grapes flat in a plastic seal-top jar.
5. Freeze the grapes for an hour. Enjoy chilled

59. MACARONI SALAD

INGREDIENTS

- Elbow macaroni, 1 lb
- Celery, sliced, ½ cup,
- sweet onion, finely diced, ¼ cup
- Garlic, minced, 2 cloves
- Sweet bell pepper, diced finely, 1 small
- Mayonnaise, 1 ½ cups
- Dijon mustard, 2 tsp
- Apple cider vinegar, 1 tsp
- Sweet pickle relish, ¼ cup
- Sugar, 1 tsp
- Black pepper, ½ tsp
- Celery seed, ¼ tsp

DIRECTIONS

1. Combine cooled macaroni, onions, celery, and bell pepper in a big bowl.
2. In another bowl, mix together the mustard, mayonnaise, vinegar, pickle relish, salt, sugar, and celery seed, mixing well.
3. Add dressing to the macaroni mixture.
4. Chill and Serve.

60. TURKEY APPLE SALAD

INGREDIENTS

- Turkey breast, unsalted cooked, 12 oz
- Celery, 1 cup
- Red apples, medium, 3
- Onion, ½ cup
- Apple juice, 2 tbsp.
- Mayonnaise, ¼ cup

DIRECTIONS

1. Split turkey into cubes. Dice the celery with the apples; slice the onion finely.
2. Combine the turkey, celery, apple, & onion in a medium bowl.
3. Insert apple juice and mayonnaise. When well blended, stir together.
4. Chill before it's fit for serving.

61. COLORFUL CHICKEN SALAD

INGREDIENTS

- Chicken Thighs, 4 w/o Skin
- Bean sprouts, 2 handfuls
- Carrot, 1 Medium
- Onion, small, ½
- Garlic, 1 clove, chopped
- Water-black eyed beans 200 g, (rinsed & drained)
- White pepper/ black pepper to taste
- Lime juice, 1 tsp
- Olive oil, 1 tbsp.

DIRECTIONS

1. In a small pan, position the chicken thighs and cover them with water. Put to a boil for 10-15 minutes and simmer. Drain and strip the flesh from the bones while it is cold and break into tiny bits.
2. Peel the carrot & cut the strips into matchstick shapes. Slice onion finely.
3. Mix together the carrot, bean sprouts, onion, garlic & beans in a large bowl. To coat the veggies, add olive oil & lemon juice and blend.
4. Include the chicken, so mix it up again. Add black pepper to season. Serve with pitta bread, toasted.

62. ITALIAN EGGPLANT SALAD

INGREDIENTS

- Eggplant, 3 cups, cubed
- Onion, 1 small, Chopped,
- White wine vinegar, 2 tbsp.
- Garlic, 1 clove, Chopped
- Oregano, ½ tsp
- Black pepper, ¼ tsp
- Tomato, 1 medium, chopped
- Olive oil, 2 tbsp.

DIRECTIONS

1. In a saucepan, transfer the eggplants to the boiling broth.
2. Reheat to boiling; heat reduction.
3. Cover and simmer for around 10 mins, until soft; drain.
4. Place the onions and eggplant in a glass dish.
5. Mix the vinegar, garlic, and pepper together.
6. Pour over the onions and eggplant; toss.
7. Before serving, stir in the oil.

63. Summer cucumber salad

Ingredients

- Cucumbers, medium, sliced, 4
- Onion, medium, sliced, 1
- Sugar, ½ cup
- White vinegar, 1 cup
- Dill (optional)
- Water, ½ cup

Directions

1. Mix onions and cucumbers in a bowl. Add a sprig of dill.
2. In a pot, cook vinegar, sugar, and water ove3r medium-high flame till sugar is dissolved.
3. While hot, dump vinegar mixture on cucumbers and stir well. Put aside for at least 30 minutes before serving.

64. Salmon Potato Salad

Ingredients

- Salmon, 1 small tin, without bones
- Lettuce leaves, 4
- Coleslaw, 1 tbsp.
- Onion, 1
- Beetroot, 2 slices
- Red pepper, 3 rings
- watercress, 1 handful
- Potatoes, 3 smalls
- Tomato, 1 small

Directions

1. Boil the potatoes in lots of water and drain until tender.
2. Slice the Ingredients from the salad into tiny bits and toss them together.
3. On a tray, place the salad & potatoes.
4. In the center of the dish, put the coleslaw & salmon and serve.

65. Cool Crispy Cucumber Salad

Ingredients

- Fresh cucumber, sliced, 2 cups
- Caesar or Italian salad dressing, 2 tbsp
- Black pepper to taste

Directions

1. Take a medium-size bowl with cover, put in salad dressing and cucumber.
2. Cover with the lid, to coat shake well.
3. Season with fresh black pepper. Chill.
4. Best served cold.

66. Tuna Mayo Pasta Salad

Ingredients

- Pasta, 3 oz
- Tuna, 8 oz can (in spring water)
- Tomato, medium, 1 Diced
- Mayonnaise low fat, 2 tbsp.
- Onions, Chopped, 2
- Sweetcorn, canned, 2 tbsp.
- Parsley/ coriander, Chopped, for garnish
- White pepper/ black pepper to taste

Directions

1. After the Instructions on the box, cook the pasta. Drain it and place it in a bowl.
2. Drain the tuna and add the spring onions, parsley & sweetcorn together with the pasta.
3. Insert the mayonnaise & stir until it is coated.
4. Season with pepper.
5. Garnish with the tomato & some extra parsley & serve.

67. Peachy Quinoa Salad

Ingredients

- Quinoa, ⅓ cup
- Walnuts, unsalted, 2 tbsp.
- Red bell pepper, ½
- Peaches, 2 fresh
- Arugula, 2 cups
- Shallot, 1

Directions

1. Process the quinoa according to the instructions on the box.
2. Strip the bell pepper & dice the shallot. Halve the peaches and cut the pits. Sliced the walnuts.
3. Spray a skillet or grill pan loosely with cooking oil and fire over medium-high heat.
4. Add the walnuts, when finely toasted, to the hot pan for a minute or two. Remove and set aside from the pan.
5. To the pan, incorporate shallot, bell pepper, & peach halves. Cook until gently browned and tender. Withdraw from the heat.
6. Top cup arugula with half cup cooked quinoa to assemble the salad. Divide and top each salad with the remaining ingredients.
7. Serve with your own vinaigrette dressing or 2 tbsp. of Peach Basil Vinaigrette Dressing.

68. Delicious Grape Salad

Ingredients

- Grapes, 3 pounds (without seed)
- Sugar, ½ cup
- Sour cream, 8 oz
- Vanilla extract, 2 tsp
- Cream cheese, 8 oz (low fat)

Directions

1. Set out the cream cheese to soften.
2. Vertically, break the grapes in two.
3. In a medium-sized cup, add the softened cream cheese, sugar, sour cream, and vanilla.
4. Fold the grapes in.
5. Chill and serve.

69. PINEAPPLE SALAD

INGREDIENTS

- Cottage cheese, 2 cups
- Lime gelatin mix, 3 oz
- Pineapple, canned, 2 cups
- Whipped topping, 8 oz

DIRECTIONS

1. Sprinkle the dry gelatin over the cottage cheese in a medium-sized dish.
2. Mix the whipped topping, and the drained pineapple together in a wide tub.
3. Fold the topping & fruit mixture into a mixture of cottage cheese. Cover & refrigerate overnight.

70. COLESLAW

INGREDIENTS

- Mayonnaise, ¼ cup
- Cabbage, 1 cup, shredded
- Onion, ¼ cup, chopped
- Green pepper, 2 tbsp, chopped
- Carrots, ¼ cup, shredded
- Sugar, 1 tbsp
- Black pepper, ½ tsp
- Vinegar, 2 tbsp
- Celery seed, ½ tsp (optional)
- Dill weeds, ⅛ tsp (optional)

DIRECTIONS

1. Mix all vegetables.
2. Whisk together mayonnaise, seasonings, and vinegar.
3. Dump over vegetables and mix.

71. Apple Caramel Salad

Ingredients

- Granny Smith apples, 3 cups
- Butterscotch dessert topping, ½ cup
- Pineapple, chopped, 8 oz can
- Butterscotch baking chips, ¼ cup
- Whipped topping, 8 oz
- Peanut, unsalted, ⅓ cup

Directions

1. Clean the apples without peeling. Cut them into cubes of around 1". Thaw the whipped topping.
2. Mix the smashed pineapple with the diced apples (including the juice).
3. Combine the thawed topping (non-dairy) in a different bowl with the butterscotch colored dessert topping till uniformly distributed.
4. In the non-dairy topping mixture, stir the apple/pineapple combination.
5. Add unsalted peanuts & butterscotch chips to the mixture.
6. Stir and serve.

72. Tuna Veggie Salad

Ingredients

- Tuna, 5 oz, can-packed in water
- Garlic, 1 clove
- Olive oil, 1 tbsp
- Bell pepper, red, ½ cup
- Zucchini, 1 cup
- Green bell pepper, ½ cup
- Green onions, ¼ cup
- Fresh basil, ¼ cup
- Red wine vinegar, 2 ½ tbsp
- Black pepper, ⅛ tsp

Directions

1. Thinly slice zucchini and Dice bell peppers. Chop basil and green onions. Mince garlic.
2. Into a medium saucepan, pour ¾ cup of water
3. Place sliced zucchini and diced bell peppers into a steamer basket and place over a saucepan filled with water. Boil water and steam veggies for 10 minutes.
4. Take off vegetables from heat, transfer to a medium serving bowl, draining off any extra water.
5. Add the green onions, basil, and tuna. Toss to mix all ingredients.
6. Combine oil, vinegar, black pepper, and garlic in a jar with a tight cover and shake it well to make the dressing.
7. Drizzle dressing over vegetable and tuna mixture and combine well.

CHAPTER 9

Main Meals

73. Basil Mince Chicken

Ingredients

- Minced chicken, 500 g
- Garlic clove, 1 crushed
- Chili, 1 chopped
- Onion, 1 chopped
- Chopped fresh basil, 1 handful
- Soy sauce, reduced-salt, 1 tbsp.
- Vegetable oil, 1 tbsp.

Directions

1. Gently heat the oil and cook the garlic and chili.
2. On a high flame, insert the mince & stir fry.
3. Include the remaining Ingredients, cover & cook gently for 15 to 20 mins or until the mince is thoroughly browned.
4. Serve with your choice of rice or pasta & a salad or a cooked vegetable.

74. Sea King Quesadilla

Ingredients

- Raw shrimp, 5 oz
- Flour tortillas, 2 (burrito size)
- Cilantro, 2 tbsp.
- Lemon juice, 1 tbsp.
- Sour cream, 2 tbsp.
- Salsa, 4 tsp
- Ground cumin, ¼ tsp
- Cayenne pepper, 1/8 tsp
- Shredded jalapeno, 2 tbsp.
- Cheddar cheese

Directions

1. Devein and shell shrimp. Rinse and cut into bite-size pieces. Chop cilantro.
2. In a zip-lock container, combine lemon juice, cilantro, cumin & cayenne pepper to make the marinade. Add the pieces of shrimp & set them aside to marinate for five minutes.
3. Heat a pan over medium heat and apply the marinade with shrimp. Stir-fry the shrimp for 1 to 2 minutes before it turns orange. Remove the fire from the pan and spoon out the shrimp, leaving the marinade.
4. To marinate in the skillet, apply the sour cream and whisk to blend.
5. Cook the tortillas in a major microwave or skillet. Spread each tortilla with 2 tsp of salsa. Cover with a combination of ½ shrimp and scatter with 1 tbsp of cheese.
6. Spoon 1 tbsp of sour cream on top of the shrimp marinade mixture. Fold the tortilla in half, heat it up in the skillet, and extract it from the pan. Repeat for the second tortilla and the shrimp, cheese & marinade left.
7. Slice the tortilla into 4 bits each. When ready to serve, garnish it with cilantro & lemon wedge.

75. CURRIED TURKEY AND RICE

INGREDIENTS

- Vegetable oil, 1 tsp
- Chopped onion, 1
- Turkey breast cut into 8 cutlets (1 pound)
- Margarine (unsalted), 1 tbsp.
- Chicken broth low sodium, 1 cup
- Curry powder, 2 tsp
- Flour, 2 tbsp.
- Creamer(non-dairy), ½ cup
- Sugar, 1 tsp
- White rice (cooked), 2 cups

DIRECTIONS

1. Heat the oil in a large skillet. Include turkey. Cook, rotating once until there is no pinker, for ten minutes, approximately. Set the turkey on a tray. To keep it warm, cover with foil.
2. Melt the margarine in the same skillet. Apply powder of onion & curry. Stirring to cook for five mins. Add flour when continually stirring.
3. Using broth, non-dairy creamer & sugar to blend. Stir regularly until the mixture thickens.
4. Send the turkey back to the skillet. Cook, turn to coat until thoroughly heated, around 2 mins.
5. Serve surrounded by white rice with turkey and sauce.

76. COCONUT CURRY NOODLE BOWL

INGREDIENTS

- Coconut oil, 2 tbsp.
- Diced onion, 1
- Rice noodles, 8 oz
- Coconut milk (full fat), 1 can
- Diced zucchini, 2
- Sweet corn kernels, 2 ears
- Thai red curry pastes, 3 tbsp.
- Minced garlic, 2 cloves
- Minced ginger, 1 tbsp.
- Water, ½-⅓ cup
- Soy sauce, 1 tbsp. (low sodium)
- Honey, 2 tsp
- Lime juice, 1 tbsp.
- For garnish
- Basil /chopped cilantro, ¼ cup
- Chopped green onions / sliced jalapeño pepper

DIRECTIONS

1. Process the rice noodles as instructed on the box.
2. In a large skillet, heat the coconut oil. Include the onion & cook for around 5 mins, over high heat. Include the zucchini, garlic, corn, and ginger and simmer for another 5 minutes or so before it all begins to soften.
3. Stir in the paste with the curry and simmer for another minute.
4. Add coconut milk, water, soy sauce, and honey to the mixture. Optional: Introduce shrimp sauté. Put to a boil and simmer (about five minutes) before the mixture starts to thicken. When the sauce gets too thick, you should add more water.
5. Withdraw the skillet from the flame. Apply either cilantro or basil and stir in the lime zest and juice, relying on the taste.
6. Divide the noodles into different bowls for serving and top with a mixture of curry. Optional: Top with green onions and jalapeño peppers, to taste.

77. Herb Rice Casserole

Ingredients

- Chicken stock, unsalted, 2 cup
- Green onions, chopped, 3
- Green bell pepper, chopped, ¼ cup
- White rice, uncooked, 1 cup
- Chives, 1 tbsp.
- Parsley flakes, ½ tsp
- Vegetable oil, 1 tbsp.

Directions

1. Preheat the oven to 350 F.
2. Add all Ingredients & place them in a casserole dish.
3. Bake for 45-50 mins in a sealed casserole or until the water is absorbed.

78. Easy Chicken Tikka

Ingredients

- Chicken breasts, 2, boneless and skinless
- Natural yogurt, low fat, 3 tbsp.
- Indian Curry paste, 1 tbsp.
- Lemon juice, 1 tsp

Directions

1. Stir in the yogurt with the curry paste.
2. In a shallow dish, place the chicken and add lemon juice & curried yogurt.
3. To enable the flavors to infuse, leave for 1 hr. or overnight in the refrigerator if you have time.
4. Cook the coated chicken for around 20 minutes under a preheated grill or until the juices run transparently when penetrated with a knife.
5. For a snack meal, represent in a tortilla wrap with shredded lettuce or serve the main meal with boiled rice & side salad.

79. Easy Turkey Burgers

Ingredients

- Onion, chopped, 1
- Minced chicken breasts, 500 g
- Black pepper to taste
- A pinch of dried mixed herbs

Directions

1. Preheat the grill or barbecue. In a large bowl, place all ingredients and mix them together.
2. Split it up into 8 small or 4 wide quantities with tidy, wet hands. To ensure even and comprehensive cooking, form the beef into flattish rounds of similar depth.
3. On each side, grill on the barbecue for 5 to10 mins.
4. The burgers must be brown, both in the middle and on the outside. Serve with a tsp of mayonnaise, mustard or tomato sauce, and shredded lettuce on a pitta bread or burger bun.

80. Seafood A La Supreme

Ingredients

- Crabmeat, 1 cup, cooked (boiled)
- Shrimp, 1 cup, cooked (boiled)
- Celery, 1 cup, chopped
- Mayonnaise, ½ cup
- Green pepper, 4 tbsp, chopped
- Green onions, 2 tbsp, chopped
- Green peas, ½ cup, frozen
- Black pepper, ½ tsp
- Bread crumbs, 1 cup

Directions

1. Heat oven to 375°f.
2. Mix all Ingredients leaving the bread crumbs in a large bowl.
3. Put this mixture in a casserole dish greased with oil.
4. Sprinkle with bread crumbs.
5. Bake casserole for 30 minutes.

81. Crispy Chicken Wraps

Ingredients

- Celery, 1 stalk
- Carrots, 1 medium
- Red bell pepper, ½
- Wheat lavash, 2 whole
- Chicken, canned, low-sodium, 8 oz
- Mayonnaise, low-fat, ¼ cup
- Onion powder, ½ tsp

Directions

1. Dice celery, bell pepper, and carrot.
2. In a shallow bowl, mix the mayonnaise and the onion powder.
3. Spread two tbsp. of the mixture on each lava flatbread.
4. Mix the diced veggies in a separate bowl.
5. Place one side of each flatbread with half of the veggies and Four oz of the chicken.
6. Roll the flatbread up and diagonally split each one in ½. With a toothpick, secure each portion.
7. Use a toothpick to hold each half of the tortilla and split each tortilla roll in two.

82. Coconut Creamy Fish

Ingredients

- Margarine/butter, low salt, 3 tsp
- Vegetable oil, 1 tbsp.
- Onion, grated, 1
- Garam masala, ¼ tsp
- Cumin seeds, 1 tsp
- Cod fillet cut into large chunks, skinless, 450 g
- Tomatoes diced, 2
- Red chili powder, ½ tsp
- Coconut milk, reduced-fat, 300 ml
- Green chilies chopped, 2 or 3
- Coriander, chopped handful
- Ground turmeric, ½ tsp

Directions

1. In a saucepan, heat the oil & margarine/butter on low heat.
2. Add the onion and the cumin seeds & fry gently until tender. . Add green chilies, tomatoes, chili powder, & ground turmeric. Stir it well.
3. Add a pinch of garam masala & stir in the coconut milk when the sauce is bright, and the oil has been separated. Stir in the cod, cover & simmer for around 12-15 minutes. To garnish, sprinkle with a bunch of coriander.
4. Serve with rice & a green salad using a spoon.

83. Thanksgiving Turkey Roast

Ingredients

- Turkey, 12 pounds (avoid self-basting), fresh or frozen
- Turkey stock, 1 cup, low-sodium (from turkey giblets)
- Fresh sage, 4 sprigs
- Fresh thyme, 3 sprigs
- Poultry seasoning, 1 tsp
- Fresh parsley, 4 sprigs
- Unsalted butter, ½ cup
- Fresh rosemary, 4 sprigs

Directions

1. Defrost the turkey in the fridge for three days before roasting. Verify to assess the cooking period, plastic wrap on the turkey.
2. Heat the furnace to 425 ° f.
3. Remove the neck and giblet pocket. Wash the turkey with tap water, and then dry with paper towels.
4. Rub the turkey flesh under the skin with poultry seasoning after unsticking the turkey breast's skin and drumsticks with your fingers. Between the turkey skin and the flesh, put the parsley, rosemary, sage, and thyme sprigs.
5. In the thickest part of the thigh, put in a meat thermometer, avoiding the bone.
6. Oil or butter the turkey and put its breast part up on a rack in a roasting pan. With aluminum foil, cover it loosely. Roast for at least 35 minutes and then decrease the heat to 330 degrees f.
7. Continue basting the turkey every 15 to 20 minutes with stock and pan juices. Take off the foil from the roasting pan in the last 30 minutes. Roast till the food thermometer records 165 ° f for 3 to 4 hours.
8. Before carving, let the roasted turkey rest for 30 minutes.

84. Ivory Coast Fish

Ingredients

- White fish fillets, medium, 2
- Onion chopped 1
- Stock cube, reduced salt 1
- Aubergines, diced 2
- Tomato puree 1 tbsp.
- Hot chili pepper 1
- Garlic, crushed 5 cloves

Directions

1. Position the aubergine in a broad cold-water tub.
2. Simmer for ten mins and Bring to boil. Drain the water and discard it.
3. In a large pot, place all the ingredients except the stock cube.
4. Cover with water & simmer for 45 mins. Insert the stock cube and begin to boil until the soup has decreased and is thick, uncovered.
5. Serve with simple boiled rice, using a spoon.

85. Chicken Stroganoff with Egg Noodles

Ingredients

- Onions, 1 cup, finely diced
- Egg, beaten, 1
- Worcestershire sauce, 2 tbsp, reduced-sodium
- Sour cream, ¼ cup
- 2 tbsp chives
- Wide egg noodles, ½ package (12 oz package), cooked
- Tomato sauce, 1 tbsp, no salt added
- Ground beef, 1 pound
- Canola oil, 3 tbsp
- Better than bouillon beef, 4 tsp, reduced-sodium
- Butter, unsalted, 2 tbsp, cold and cubed
- Breadcrumbs, ¼ cup
- Mayonnaise, 1 tbsp
- Flour, 2 tbsp
- Water, 3 cups
- Black pepper, 1 tsp, freshly ground
- Parsley, ¼ cup
- Rosemary, chopped, 1 tbsp

Directions

1. Mix the onion, Worcestershire sauce, egg, breadcrumbs, mayonnaise, tomato sauce, and half tsp black pepper in a big bowl. Include the ground beef and mix thoroughly. Make 15 meatballs of the same size.
2. Cook stroganoff meatballs in a big frypan until browned on medium heat. Shift all meatballs to another pan. Add oil and flour to the big fry pan and stir till well-combined. Add the remaining black pepper, water, and bouillon. Add in the fried meatballs and then keep stirring until sauce thickens for 10 minutes.
3. Take off the heat and mix in chives and sour cream, then top over egg noodles.

Pasta:
4. Into a large wok/pan, add egg noodles with 2 tbsp of hot water and stir until warm, then take off the heat. Add in butter, rosemary and parsley until everything is well incorporated.

86. Easy low sodium Lemon chicken

Ingredients

- Chicken breasts, 4, boneless skinless ½" thickness
- Vegetable oil 1 tbsp
- White wine ⅓ cup
- Lemon juice 2 tbsp
- Dried oregano 2 tbsp
- Lemon, sliced 1
- Black pepper, fresh ground ½ tsp

Directions

1. Heat a frying pan for approximately 2 minutes over medium/high heat. Add oil and wine and lemon juice.
2. Put the chicken breasts in the skillet, sprinkle ½ the oregano and half the pepper, and cook for 3-4 mins. Rotate the breasts and sprinkle with the remaining oregano & pepper and cook 3-4 minutes more. With an instant-read thermometer, the internal temp must be 165 F. Remove the chicken and set it aside.
3. Apply lemon slices to the pan and liquid & continue to heat until the lemons tend to caramelize for a few minutes. Then lower the heat to boil until about half the mixture decreases.
4. Serve over the chicken with the sauce & lemons poured with the pan.

87. Easy low sodium salmon with lime and herbs

Ingredients

- Salmon fillets, 4
- Limes, 2
- Fresh thyme, 12 springs
- Fresh dill weed, 2 tsp / dried and crumbled 1 tsp

Directions

1. On a complete sheet of aluminum foil, put 2 salmon fillets each (enough foil to wrap across fillets with space to spare carefully). Squeeze 1 lime juice over the fish and rub with dillweed carefully.
2. Slice the 2nd lime thinly and put over fish slices. Put thyme sprigs on top and fold aluminum foil over gently to make pouches.
3. Put pouches on the grill for approximately 12-15 minutes over medium heat, rotating once every 7 minutes. When finished, the fish will slough with a fork.

88. Low sodium pumpkin soup

Ingredients

- Pumpkin puree, one can, (15 oz)
- Onion, chopped, 1 small
- Vegetable broth unsalted, 2 cups
- Ground cinnamon, ½ tsp
- Ground nutmeg, ¼ tsp
- Ground pepper, ¼ tsp
- Skim milk, 1 cup
- Water, ¾ cup divided

Directions

1. Add ¼ cup of water to a wide saucepan & heat over a moderate flame to boil. Add the onion, then simmer for three minutes.
2. Add the remaining water, vegetable broth (pumpkin puree), cinnamon, nutmeg & pepper. When getting it to a simmer, stir well. Reduce the flame and leave for 5 minutes to simmer. Add the milk and hold simmering for ten minutes.

89. Easy Chicken Fajitas

Ingredients

- Vegetable oil 2 tbsp
- Chicken strips raw 1 ½ pound
- Chili powder 2 tsp
- Cumin ½ tsp
- Lemon or lime juice 2 tbsp
- Green and red pepper, ¼ sliced lengthwise
- Onion white, ½ sliced lengthwise
- Dry cilantro ½ tsp
- Flour tortillas 4
- Vegetable spray

Directions

1. Preheat the oven to 300 F.
2. Apply the vegetable oil over medium heat to a non-stick frying pan.
3. Add the meat, seasonings, & lemon/lime juice; cook until tender or for 5-10 minutes.
4. Add the onion and pepper to the skillet and simmer for 1-2 minutes.
5. Remove from heat; whisk in cilantro.
6. Place the tortillas on the foil and move them to the oven. 10 minutes of heat
7. Divide the mixture into tortillas, wrap them, and serve them.

90. Chicken and Pesto Pasta

Ingredients

- Broccoli head, ½, Cut in small florets
- Chicken breasts, 2 small (or 200 g cut in strips)
- Crème Fraiche (low fat), 4 tbsp
- Green pesto, 2 tbsp.
- Twirl dried pasta, 150 g

Directions

1. Break the chicken into strips, which are 1 cm thick. Stir-fry for 2-3 minutes in a non-stick pan before the chicken starts to tan. Attach the crème Fraiche & pesto and cover. Cook for 5-10 more minutes on low heat before the chicken is cooked through.
2. Meanwhile, according to the box's guidance, cook the pasta and introduce the broccoli for the last five mins of cooking.
3. Drain the pasta & broccoli well & combine with the chicken & pesto that have been cooked. Serve.

91. LIME BAKED FISH

INGREDIENTS

- White fish fillets, boneless 4 x 100 g portions
- Lime juice 2 tbsp.
- Butter/margarine, unsalted 1 tbsp.
- Drill black pepper /dried rosemary, 1 pinch
- Zest of one lime

DIRECTIONS

1. Preheat the oven to the gas mark 4/ 180 ° C/350 ° F/.
2. In a baking dish, place the fish in one single layer. The butter/margarine, grated lemon rind, lemon juice, rosemary, & pepper are blended and scattered over the fish fillets.
3. Wrap in foil & bake for 25 mins or fish flakes easily on tested with a fork.
4. Serve with your favorite boiled/mashed potatoes/rice a boiled vegetable.

92. STIR FRY MEAL

INGREDIENTS

- Cooking oil 2 tbsp
- Chicken breast, 2 media, cut in bite-size pieces
- Frozen stir fry vegetables 1 10-oz package
- Soy sauce, low sodium ½ tbsp
- Cooked rice 2 cups

DIRECTIONS

1. Heat oil in a 9-10 'high skillet.
2. Introduce and sauté the chicken.
3. Use vegetables to stir.
4. Mix well and apply soy sauce.
5. Reduce heat to medium and simmer for 3-5 minutes uncovered, or until cooked with frequent stirring.
6. Serving with 2/3 cups of rice.

93. TURKEY & NOODLES

INGREDIENTS

- Lean ground turkey, 2 pounds fresh
- Elbow macaroni, 2 cups dry
- Vegetable, 1 tbsp
- Regular tomatoes, 1 14-oz can, diced
- Green onions, ½ cup, chopped
- Green pepper, ½ cup, chopped
- Italian seasoning, 1 tbsp
- Black pepper, 1 tsp

DIRECTIONS

1. Start by boiling water in a large boiler, add macaroni. Let boil until desired tenderness or for 5 minutes. Drain macaroni and put aside.
2. In a large skillet, heat veg. Oil on medium heat. In heated oil, add ground turkey, stirring occasionally, and cook until done.
3. Add diced tomatoes, green peppers, onions, black pepper, Italian seasoning, and cooked macaroni. Combine well.
4. Cover and cook for further 5 minutes. Serve warm.

94. BBQ CUPS

INGREDIENTS

- Spicy barbecue sauce ½ cup
- Ground turkey, ¾ pounds lean
- Garlic powder, dash
- Onion flakes, 2 tsp
- Refrigerator biscuits, low-fat, 1 10-oz package

DIRECTIONS

1. In a nonstick skillet, cook turkey until brown.
2. Add garlic powder, barbecue sauce, and onion flakes. Combine well.
3. Grease muffin tins, flatten one biscuit and push into muffin tin one at a time.
4. Add the beef mixture with a spoon into each biscuit cup's center.
5. Bake for 10 to 12 minutes at 400°f.

95. Crispy Oven Baked Chicken

Ingredients

- Fryer chicken, 2 ½ pounds, (cut as desired)
- Corn flakes, 1 cup, crushed
- All-purpose flour, 1 cup
- Lemon juice, 1 tbsp
- Black pepper, 1 tsp
- Poultry seasoning, ¼ tsp
- Vegetable oil, 4 tbsp

Directions

1. Heat oven to 400°F.
2. Rinse chicken pieces thoroughly and dry with a kitchen towel; massage with lemon juice.
3. Mix flour, corn flakes, poultry seasoning, and black pepper in a small bag.
4. Shake thoroughly.
5. Grease a shallow baking tray (about "deep) with vegetable oil.
6. Put the chicken in the bag of flour and seasoning mixture; put in the large pieces first. Shake thoroughly.
7. Put the coated chicken in the greased pan.
8. Bake for 20-30 minutes on each side until brown.

96. Stuffed Red Peppers 96. Stuffed Red Peppers

Ingredients

- Red peppers, 6 smalls, seeded with tops removed
- Cooked rice, 1 ½ cups
- Turkey, ½ pound ground and lean (or chicken)
- Onions, ¼ cup, chopped
- Celery, ¼ cup, chopped
- Italian seasoning, 2 tbsp
- Lemon juice, 2 tbsp
- Black pepper, 1 tsp
- Sugar, ½ tsp
- Celery seed, 1 tbsp
- Paprika
- Vegetable oil, 2 tbsp

Directions

1. Heat oven to 325°F.
2. In a saucepan, heat oil.
3. Add onions, ground meat, and celery; cook till meat is good and brown.
4. Include all ingredients in a saucepan, leaving paprika and green peppers. Mix, take off from the heat.
5. Fill the peppers with the cooked mixture. Put foil over it or put it in a baking dish and cover.
6. Bake for around 30 minutes. Take out and season with paprika.

97. Spicy Jalapeño Pepper Chicken

Ingredients

- Chicken, cut up, 2-3 pounds (skin and fat removed)
- Chicken bouillon, low-sodium, 1 ½ cups
- Ground nutmeg, ½ tsp
- Black pepper, ¼ tsp
- Onion, 1, sliced into rings
- Jalapeño peppers, 2 tsp, fresh, chopped finely, and seeded
- Vegetable oil, 3 tbsp

Directions

1. Put a big skillet on medium-high heat with oil and cook the chicken pieces till brown. Put aside, keep it warm.
2. Sauté onion rings in hot oil. Put in bouillon and bring it to a boil, stirring frequently.
3. Put chicken back in pan; add black pepper and nutmeg. Top with lid and simmer until chicken is soft or for 35 minutes.
4. Mix in jalapeño peppers, and cook on low for another minute.

98. Cod with Cilantro-Lime

Ingredients

- Cod fillets, 1 pound
- Mayonnaise, ½ cup
- Lime juice, 2 tbsp
- Fresh cilantro, ½ cup

Directions

1. Combine mayonnaise, lime juice, and chopped cilantro in a medium bowl. Separate ¼ cup of the sauce into a small bowl and put aside to serve with the fish.
2. Coat fish with the remaining mayonnaise mixture.
3. With a nonstick cooking spray, spray a large skillet and heat on medium-high heat. Put cod fillets in it and cook both sides, turning once until fish is moist but firm for about 8 minutes.
4. Serve with remainder cilantro-lime sauce.

99. CHICKEN NUGGETS WITH SAUCE

INGREDIENTS

- Chicken breasts, 1 pound, boneless
- Egg, 1 large
- Low-fat milk, 1%, 2 tbsp
- Yellow mustard, 1 tbsp
- Mayonnaise, ½ cup
- Honey, ⅓ cup
- Worcestershire sauce, 2 tsp
- Cornflakes, 3 cups

DIRECTIONS

1. In a small bowl, stir the mayonnaise, mustard, Worcestershire sauce, and honey. Chill the sauce in a Refrigerator till the nuggets are done, then use it as a dipping sauce.
2. Heat the oven to 400° F.
3. Slice the breast pieces into 36 same-sized pieces.
4. Squash the cornflakes and transfer the crumbs into a big zip-lock bag.
5. Take a small mixing bowl, beat the egg, and then mix it with milk. Dunk the small chicken pieces in the whisked egg, then put them in a Ziploc bag and shake to coat with the cornflake crumbs.
6. On the baking tray sprayed with nonstick cooking spray, Put the nuggets and bake for 15 minutes or until tender.

100. INDIAN CHICKEN DRUMSTICK CURRY

INGREDIENTS

- Chicken drumsticks, small, 1-½ pounds
- Cayenne pepper, 1-½ tsp
- Garam masala, ½ tsp
- Tomato, 1 medium
- Onions, 2 mediums
- Garlic, 2 cloves
- Ginger root, 1 cube
- Whole cumin seeds, ¾ tsp
- Cinnamon stick, 1
- Bay leaves, 2
- Whole peppercorns, ¼ tsp
- Salt, ¾ tsp
- Vegetable oil, 5 tbsp

DIRECTIONS

1. Peel the tomato and chop. Mince the garlic, ginger root, and onion. Take off and discard the skin from the chicken.
2. Heat the oil in a wide, large pot on medium-high flame. Add to it the cumin seeds, bay leaves, cinnamon stick, and peppercorns. Stirring once.
3. Also, add the garlic, ginger, and onion. Stir these Ingredients till the onion gets brown specks.
4. To it, add the chicken, tomato, cayenne pepper, salt, and ¼ cup water. Stir and take to a boil.
5. Put on the lid on the pot tightly, reduce the heat, and simmer for about 25 minutes on low heat or till the chicken is soft and tender. Stirring in between the cooking period.
6. Take off the cover and increase heat to medium. Season with garam masala and stirring gently, cook to decrease the liquid for about 5 minutes.

101. Chicken and Summer Vegetable Kebabs

Ingredients

- Chicken thighs, boneless, skinless, 1 pound
- Zucchini, 1 medium
- Summer squash, 1 medium, yellow
- Bell pepper, 1 red
- Onion, 1 medium
- Olive oil, 2 tbsp
- Peach jam, 1 tbsp
- Lemon juice, 2 tbsp
- Herb seasoning blend, 1 tsp
- Salt, ¼ tsp

Directions

1. Into a small microwave-safe bowl, measure the peach jam to make the marinade by heating for 10 to 15 seconds in the microwave to liquefy. Include the herb seasoning with olive oil, lemon juice, and salt. Mix well until blended.
2. Wash the chicken thighs, and with a paper towel, pat dry. Chop each boneless thigh into 4 pieces and put them in a zip-lock bag.
3. Add half of the marinade to the boneless pieces (the remaining half of the marinade to be used on the veggies.) Close the zip-lock bag and put it in the fridge to marinate.
4. Slice the veggies into small-sized pieces to make kebabs. Put them in a container and add the remaining marinade. Mix to coat the veggies.
5. Thread the chicken pieces and vegetables onto skewers (8 small or 4 large skewers).
6. On a Heated medium grill, place the skewers and cook with cover for 12 to 15 minutes. To cook evenly, turn the skewers frequently.

102. Turkey Sloppy Joes

Ingredients

- Hamburger buns, 6
- Ground turkey, 7% fat, 1-½ pounds
- Bell pepper green, ½ cup
- Chicken grilling seasoning blend, 1 tbsp
- Red onion, ½ cup
- Worcestershire sauce, 1 tbsp
- Tomato sauce, low-sodium, 1 cup,
- Brown sugar, 2 tbsp

Directions

1. Chop the bell pepper and onion.
2. In a large skillet, Place the vegetables with ground turkey and cook on medium-high till turkey is thoroughly cooked. Do not drain the liquid.
3. Mix the brown sugar, grilling seasoning, tomato sauce, and Worcestershire sauce in a small bowl.
4. Add the above sauce to the meat mixture. Lower heat and simmer for 10 minutes.
5. Split turkey mixture into six parts and serve on burger buns.

103. Baked fish

Ingredients

- Green pepper, ¼ medium
- Lemon, 1 small
- Trout fillets, 4 3-oz (or any other baking fish)
- Paprika, 1 ½ tsp
- Black pepper, 1 ½ tsp
- Garlic powder, 1 tbsp
- Onion, 1 small
- Parmesan cheese, 2 tbsp

Directions

1. Heat oven to 375°f.
2. In a greased baking tray, Place fish on an aluminum foil.
3. On both sides of the fish, sprinkle garlic powder, black pepper, and paprika.
4. Place Cut green peppers on fish. Also, place sliced onion rings on fish.
5. Pour lemon juice on fish.
6. Bake for at least 30 minutes.
7. After the fish has baked, scatter with parmesan cheese. Enjoy hot.

104. Chicken and Pasta Easy Dinner

Ingredients

- Vegetables, ⅔ cup
- Chicken breast, cooked, 5 oz
- Zucchini 1 cup
- Red bell pepper ½ cup
- Olive oil 1 tbsp
- Pasta, any shape cooked 2 cups
- Italian dressing low-sodium 3 tbsp

Directions

1. Slice bell pepper and zucchini.
2. Take a nonstick pan, heat the olive oil, sauté peppers, and zucchini until crispy tender. Take out on a plate.
3. Cut meat into strips.
4. Heat chicken strips and cooked pasta in the microwave one by one.
5. Mix pasta with dressing. Dish out with chicken strips and sautéed vegetables.

105. Ginger Orange Chicken

Ingredients

- Chicken breasts/legs, skinless, 4
- Orange juice, 3 tbsp.
- Honey 1 tbsp.
- Mustard 1 tbsp.
- Ginger powder, Ground 2 tsp

Directions

1. Preheat oven to 375 degrees F/ 190 degrees C / Gas Mark 5. Make three cuts/scores per piece of chicken and put them in a casserole dish or roasting tin.
2. Mix the honey, mustard, orange juice, ground ginger, and orange zest & spoon over the chicken.
3. Cook for 25-30 minutes in the preheated oven, or until completely cooked.
4. Serve with your option of boiled fresh potatoes, rice or crusty bread, and boiled vegetables.

106. One-Pot Tuna Dinner

Ingredients

- Albacore tuna, 1 9 ¼-oz low sodium, with water, drained
- Cooked rotini, 2 cups hot, (, cooked without salt or fat corkscrew pasta,)
- Vegetable cooking spray
- Fresh onion, 2 tbsp minced
- Black pepper, ¼ tsp
- Cream of mushroom soup, low sodium, 1 10 ¾-oz can, undiluted
- Water, ⅔ cup
- Curry powder, ¼ tsp
- Green peas, ½ cup frozen, thawed
- Fresh parsley chopped (optional)

Directions

1. Coat with cooking spray a large nonstick skillet; position over moderate heat.
2. Add in onion; fry until soft.
3. In a bowl, mix the water, soup, pepper and, curry powder; whisk well and transfer to the skillet.
4. Add the cooked peas, rotini, and tuna; combine properly. Cook without covering, for 10 minutes over low heat, Occasional stirring.
5. If needed, garnish with parsley.

107. Shrimp with Crab filling

Ingredients

- Jumbo shrimp, 12, raw and shelled with tails on
- Crab meat, 6 oz
- Dry bread crumbs, ¼ cup
- Unsalted butter, 3 tbsp
- Celery, 1 tsp
- Parsley, 1 tsp
- Lemon juice, ¼ tsp
- Hot sauce, 3 drops
- Onion, 1 tsp
- Green bell pepper, 1 tsp
- Garlic powder, ⅛ tsp
- Black pepper, ⅛ tsp

Directions

1. Heat the 450 ° F oven.
2. Finely chop the parsley, celery, bell pepper, onion, and crab meat.
3. In a bowl, combine bread crumbs, crab, 3 tbsp of melted butter, parsley, celery, bell pepper, and onion; put aside.
4. Use a nonstick cooking spray to spray a baking dish.
5. Devein and clean the shrimp, and pat it off. (Frozen shrimps may be used -thaw before using in the recipe.)
6. Using a sharp knife to remove a ½"- deep pocket from the tail around the middle of the shrimp's inner curved side, leave ½ "at the edge. Do not touch the shrimp's back. Using your finger to enlarge the pocket.
7. Use about 2-½ tbsp per shrimp of the crab mixture. Position the crab in the shrimp pocket and spread it to fill. On a baking sheet, place the shrimp. Repeat. Prepare all the shrimp.
8. Brush the melting butter on the shrimp. For 10 to 12 minutes, bake. Don't overcook it.
9. When needed, serve with melted, unsalted butter.

108. Oven-Fried Crunchy Catfish

Ingredients

- Catfish fillets, 1 pound
- Egg white, 1
- Cajun seasoning, salt-free, 1 tsp
- All-purpose flour, ½ cup
- Cornmeal, ¼ cup
- Bread crumbs, panko, ¼ cup

Directions

1. Preheat oven to 450° F.
2. Spray with nonstick cooking spray on the top of a flat, nonstick baking tray.
3. In a shallow bowl, beat the egg whites till very soft peaks form. Try not to over-beat.
4. Sprinkle flour on a wax paper sheet.
5. Combine the panko, cornmeal, and Cajun seasoning on another wax paper sheet.
6. Divide catfish fillet into a total of four portions. Submerge the fish into the flour and shake off extra.
7. Then dip in the whisked egg white.
8. And roll in the mixture of cornmeal.
9. Place coated fish on the baking tray and go over steps 6 to 9 with all fillets.
10. With cooking spray, spray-on tops of the fish fillets and bake for about 10 to 12 minutes, till the fish fillets are browned and sizzling. Take out the pan from the oven and turn the fish to the other side.
11. Put back in the oven and more bake for 5 minutes until fillets are crisp and browned.

109. Garlic and Shrimp Linguine

Ingredients

- Raw shrimp, ¾ pound
- Linguine, uncooked, 12 oz
- Flat-leaf parsley, 1 cup
- Water, 2 ½ quarts
- Olive oil, 2 tbsp

- Garlic, 2 heads whole
- Lemon juice, 1 tbsp
- Black pepper, ¼ tsp

Directions

1. Clean and Peel shrimp. Chop the parsley.
2. In a large pot, boil water. Include pasta and boil until tender or for 10 minutes.
3. When pasta is cooking, separate the garlic cloves with skin on. Fry cloves in a pan on medium heat, stirring constantly. When it becomes soft to touch and darkens, the garlic is ready. Skin will remove easily. Remove from pan and peel the skin.
4. In a sauté pan, heat olive oil, and put back peeled garlic in the pan. Fry garlic till golden.
5. Add shrimp and parsley and cook for 1 to 2 minutes till shrimp becomes pink.
6. Draining pasta, reserve 1 cup of liquid. Add drained pasta to the frying pan with garlic and shrimp. Combine all ingredients and add the reserved liquid to it.
7. Add black pepper and lemon juice. Stir and serve.

110. Chicken and Veggie Stew

Ingredients

- Fresh okra, 2 cups sliced
- Whole chicken, 1 skinless (cut in pieces)
- Ginger, 1 piece
- Onion, ½
- Vegetable oil, 1 tbsp.
- Onion, chopped, 1

- Tomatoes, chopped, 2
- Peanut butter, 2 tbsp.
- Hot chilies, 2 chopped / cayenne pepper, 1 tsp
- Eggplant, 1 (peeled & cubed)

Directions

1. In a big bowl of water, soak the okra & eggplant for 1to 2 hours. Drain.
2. Boil the pieces of chicken in two cups of water with ginger and half of the onion.
3. Heat the oil over low heat in a separate pot & fry the chopped onion until tender. Add tomatoes.
4. Take the chicken pieces that are partially cooked and return to the pot, along with approximately half of the broth.
5. Include the salt, peanut butter, cayenne pepper, and chilies. Before tossing in the drained okra & eggplant, simmer for 5 minutes.
6. Once the chicken & vegetables are tender, continue cooking.
7. To retain a thick stew consistency, add more broth as required.
8. Serve with cornflour or wheat dumplings or with rice bread.

111. Shrimp pilaf

Ingredients

- Raw shrimp, 2 pounds
- Converted (parboiled) white rice, uncooked, 2 cups
- Onion, 2 cups
- Bell pepper, 1 cup
- Garlic cloves, 2
- Black pepper, ½ tsp
- Canned low-sodium tomato sauce, 8 oz
- Low-sodium chicken broth, 2 cups
- Butter or trans-fat free margarine, ½ cup

Directions

1. Heat the oven to 350° F.
2. Chop the garlic, onion, and bell pepper coarsely. Devein, peel, and wash the shrimp.
3. Combine all the given items in a big bowl, leaving butter.
4. Into a 9" x 13" baking dish, pour the mixture and spread evenly.
5. Chop the butter into small pieces and place them on top of the mixture.
6. Cover tray with foil.
7. For 1 hour and 15 minutes, bake. Enjoy hot.

112. Chicken Stew

Ingredients

- All-purpose flour, 2 tbsp
- Chicken broth, low-sodium, 2 10 ½-oz cans
- Vegetable oil, 3 tbsp
- Chicken breast, 2 pounds, cut into bite-size pieces
- Onions, sliced, 1 cup
- Sliced okra, frozen, 1 10 oz bag
- Green peppers, ¾ cup
- Garlic, 2 cloves, minced
- Frozen carrots, 1 10 oz bag
- Dried basil, ¼ tsp
- Black pepper, ¼ tsp

Directions

1. In the Dutch oven, heat 2 tbsp of oil; put in chicken and fry on medium-high heat.
2. Take out chicken and put it aside. Add the remainder 1 tbsp of oil.
3. Include and fry the onion, garlic, and pepper.
4. Put in the flour and cook for 2 to 3 minutes, stirring frequently.
5. Add in chicken and broth, cook till it starts boiling.
6. Include carrots, black pepper, and basil, simmer covered for around 10 minutes. As it simmers, the gravy will thicken.
7. Cook after adding okra for another 5-10 minutes.
8. Dish up over steaming white rice.

113. Turkey Casserole

Ingredients

- Chicken breast, 2 pounds
- Shitake mushrooms, sliced, 1 cup
- White potato, 1 cup
- Chicken broth, low-sodium, 4 cups
- Onion, 2 cups
- Garlic, 3 cloves
- Carrots, 2 cups
- White flour, ⅓ cup, all-purpose
- Herb seasoning blend, ¾ tsp
- Olive oil, 2 tbsp
- Dried thyme, ½ tbsp
- Red wine, 1 cup, dry
- Bay leaf, 1
- Black pepper, ½ tsp

Directions

1. Peel and wash potatoes and make them into small cubes. Prepare according to lo potassium potato recipe.
2. Cut chicken into bite-sized pieces. Mince garlic cloves and chop onion. Slice carrots.
3. Heat 2 tsp olive oil in the big Dutch oven on medium-high heat.
4. Put in onions and sauté until soft; add in thyme and mushrooms; mix and sauté for 5 more minutes. Adding garlic sauté for a minute more.
5. To the mixture, add red wine and stir.
6. Dust chicken with flour. On medium heat, heat 2 tsp oil in a large frying pan. Add in half of floured chicken and season with 1/8 tsp of seasoning blend. Keep cooking until all sides are browned. Repeat the process with the remainder 2 tsp oil, floured chicken, and 1/8 tsp seasoning blend.
7. To the mushroom mixture, add browned chicken.
8. Add bay leaf and broth to the mixture. Take to a boil.
9. Decrease the flame to medium-low cover and simmer until chicken is tender.
10. Take prepared low potassium potatoes. Stir in the carrots and the potatoes into the pot with the chicken. Cook on low heat to thicken sauces, stirring occasionally.
11. Season with remainder ½ tsp seasoning blend and black pepper. Take out and throw away bay leaf and serve.

115. Grilled Trout

Ingredients

- Rainbow trout fillets, 2 pounds
- Cooking oil, 1 tbsp
- Salt, ½ tsp
- Lemon pepper salt-free, 1 tsp
- Paprika, ½ tsp

Directions

1. Heat grill on high heat.
2. Spray or brush the trout fillets lightly with oil on all sides. Mix the spices in a small bowl. Rub thoroughly on the fillets.
3. Put the seasoned trout directly on the heated grill, fillet side down. Grill for 4 minutes. Brush or spray the skin with oil lightly. Turn over the fillets and cook till the fish flakes with a fork easily, around 3 to 5 minutes.
4.

116. Barley Chicken Stew

Ingredients

- Pearl barley, 1 cup, uncooked
- Onion, ½ cup
- Large stalk celery, 1
- Garlic, 1 clove
- Carrots, 2 mediums
- Chicken, boneless, 1 lb.
- White flour, 2 tbsp, all-purpose
- Black pepper, ¼ tsp
- Canola oil, 2 tbsp
- Onion herb seasoning, 1 tsp
- Bay leaves, 2
- Salt, ½ tsp

Directions

1. In 2 cups of water, immerse the barley for 1 hour.
2. Coarsely chop the celery and onion. Cut carrots into thick rounds of ¼-inch each. Grind the garlic clove. Chop the chicken into squares of 1-½ inch.
3. Put chicken, flour, and black pepper in a plastic bag. Vigorously shake to coat chicken cubes with flour.
4. In a heavy pot, heat the oil and brown the chicken.
5. Add and sauté onion, garlic, and celery for 2 minutes. Add 3 cups of water. Include bay leaves and salt, decrease heat, and simmer for 5 minutes.
6. Rinse and drain barley, then include it in the pot. Cook covered for 1 hour. Stirring every 15 minutes.
7. Add the sliced carrots after 1 hour, season with herb seasoning. Let simmer for 1 more hour. Water can be added to prevent sticking.

117. White Bean and Chicken Chili

Ingredients

- Chicken breasts, boneless,1 pound, skinless
- Chicken broth, 4 cups, low-sodium
- Onions, white pearl, 6 whole
- Black pepper, 1 tsp
- Celery, ¾ cup
- Garlic, 4 cloves
- Onion, ¾ cup
- Carrot, ¾ cup
- White beans, 1 cup, canned
- Golden hominy, 15 ½ oz (1 can)
- Green chilies, diced, 4.5 oz
- canned
- Garlic powder, 2 tsp
- Cayenne pepper, ¼ tsp
- Chili powder, 2 tsp
- Oregano, 1 tsp
- Ground cumin, 2 tsp

Directions

1. Chop the chicken into small square bits. Sprinkle with pepper and put in the crock-pot.
2. Chop the celery, carrots, and onion coarsely. Finely mince the garlic. To decrease sodium, drain and rinse the beans and hominy with ample water.
3. Add the chopped onion, carrots, garlic, celery, hominy, beans, pearl onions, chicken broth, and green chilies to the crock-Pot.
4. Add cayenne pepper, garlic powder, chili powder, cumin, and oregano.
5. Cover the lid and cook on low setting for 8 hours in the crock-Pot.

118. POT PIE CHICKEN

INGREDIENTS

- Chicken breast, 1 ½ pound, (boneless, skinless)
- Chicken stock, low-sodium, 2 cups
- Canola oil, ¼ cup
- Flour, ½ cup
- Sweet peas, frozen, ½ cup thawed
- Italian seasoning, sodium-free, 1 tbsp
- Chicken bouillon, 2 tsp (low sodium)
- Fresh carrots, ½ cup, diced
- Fresh onions, ½ cup, diced
- Fresh celery, ¼ cup diced
- Black pepper, ½ tsp
- Heavy cream, ½ cup
- Piecrust, 1 frozen, cooked and broken into bite-size pieces
- Cheddar cheese, low-fat, 1 cup

DIRECTIONS

1. Pound chicken and chop into small cubes.
2. Put chicken and stock in a large stockpot and for 30 minutes, let cook on medium-high heat. Then, blend oil and flour until mixed totally.
3. Slowly pour and mix into the chicken broth mixture till it slightly thickens. Decrease flame for 15 minutes to medium-low or low.
4. Add Italian seasoning, black pepper onions, carrots, celery, and bouillon. Cook for 15 more minutes.
5. Take off from flame and then include peas and cream. Mix until well combined. Serve in mugs and garnish with the same amounts of piecrust and cheese.

119. NAVY BEAN KIDNEY-FRIENDLY STEW

INGREDIENTS

- Onion, 1, medium chopped
- Carrots, raw, 1 cup grated
- Chicken Bouillon, 2 cups, Sodium Free
- Pepper, 2 tbsp
- Navy beans, raw, mature seeds, 1 lb, rinsed thoroughly
- Tomatoes, 2 can, packed in tomato
- juice (15 oz cans), no salt added
- Taste of Louisiana, ½ tbsp
- Garlic, 3 cloves

DIRECTIONS

1. Wash and immerse 1 lb. navy beans in ample water overnight.
2. Cook in a slow cooker with the soaked water.
3. Add in onion, garlic, tomatoes, shredded carrots, Taste of Louisiana seasoning, black pepper, and chicken stock.
4. Combine completely and cook for 6-8 hours on low heat.
5. Dish out 1 cup into a serving bowl and serve immediately.

120. Italian Chicken Pizza

Ingredients

- All-purpose flour, 2 cups
- Active dry yeast, 1 tsp
- Granulated sugar, 1 tbsp
- Vegetable shortening, 2 tbsp
- Water, 1 cup
- Ingredients for Filling:

- Chicken mince, ½ pound
- Italian seasoning, ½ tsp
- Green peppers, ½ cup, diced
- Onions, ½ cup, diced
- Chili powder, 1 tsp
- Garlic powder, ½ tsp

- Tomato paste, ¼ cup
- Onion powder, ½ tsp
- Italian seasoning, 1 tsp
- Water, ½ cup
- Vegetable oil, ½ cup
- Sharp cheddar cheese, 4 oz reduced fat, grated

Directions

1. Prepare pizza dough by mixing flour, sugar, and yeast.
2. Include shortening to the above mixture; mix all using a fork.
3. Include water in little by little, while mixing flour mix with the fork until it combines well together and does not stick to the bowl.
4. Let the dough rest, covered for about 15 minutes.

Filling:

5. Heat oven to 425°f.
6. Sauté chicken mince in a frying pan. Add onion powder, Italian seasoning, and garlic powder; mix continuously until meat is browned.
7. Drain the excess oil.
8. In a small vessel, prepare the pizza sauce by mixing the tomato paste, Italian seasoning, chili powder, and water. Put aside.
9. Take the rested dough, grease the pizza pan with your fingers. Spread dough on the pan evenly by hand.
10. Evenly spread the sauce all over pizza dough; scatter with ½ cup of cheese.
11. Bake in the heated oven for around 15-20 minutes.
12. Take out from oven; include ground beef, green peppers, onions, and remaining cheese.
13. Bake again for an added 10 minutes. Serve hot.

121. Slow-Cooked Tender Chicken

Ingredients

- Chicken breast, 1 pound, boneless, skinless
- Chicken broth, ¼ cup, low sodium
- Dried oregano, 1 tsp
- Ground black pepper, ¼ tsp
- Butter, unsalted, 2 tbsp
- Water, ¼ cup
- Lemon juice, 1 tbsp
- Garlic, minced, 2 cloves
- Fresh basil, 1 tsp, chopped

Directions

1. In a small bowl, mix oregano and grounded black pepper. Coat mixture on the chicken.
2. In a medium skillet, soften the butter over medium heat. Cook the chicken in the melted butter till it is golden brown and then shift it to the slow cooker.
3. To loosen the brown bits stuck in the skillet, pour water, chicken broth, garlic, and lemon juice in the skillet, get it to a boil. Pour this over the browned chicken.
4. Close the slow cooker and set it on low for 5 hours or on high for 2½ hours.
5. Baste chicken and Add basil. For an additional 15–30 minutes, Cover and cook on high or until chicken is soft and tender.

122. Hot n Spicy Chicken

Ingredients

- Chicken, 1 whole, cut in small parts, skin removed
- Lemon juice, ¼ cup
- Onion, 1 medium, chopped
- Garlic clove, 1 medium chopped (optional)
- Dry thyme, ½ tsp
- Curry powder, 2 tsp
- Water, 1 cup
- Black pepper, ½ tsp
- Vegetable, 2 tbsp (or olive oil)

Directions

1. Apply lemon juice on cleaned chicken; let stand for 15 minutes and wash it.
2. Combine all the spices in a small tub and rub it on chicken parts.
3. Marinate the seasoned chicken overnight in the refrigerator (can be used after 1 hour).
4. In a large pan, heat oil and fry seasoned chicken till golden.
5. Take the leftover marinade of the chicken and add water to it.
6. Put this remaining marinade over browned Chicken. Let simmer on low heat until tender.
7. Top over hot rice and serve.

123. Herbed Chicken Breast Bake

Ingredients

- Chicken breasts, 1 pound, skinless, boneless,
- Herb and garlic seasoning blend, Mrs. Dash, 2 tbsp
- Onion, 1 medium
- Garlic, 1–2 cloves
- Black pepper, 1 tsp freshly ground
- Olive oil, ¼ cup

Directions

Marination:
1. Chop onion and garlic finely and put it in a marinade bowl. Adding ground pepper, seasoning, and olive oil.
2. To the above marinade, add chicken breasts coat the marinade fully. Cover and refrigerate overnight or for at least 4 hours.

Baking:
3. Heat the oven to 360°F.
4. Set the marinated chicken on a baking tray covered with foil.
5. Dump the remaining marinade over the chicken breasts and roast for 20 minutes at 350°F.
6. Broil for browning for an additional 5 minutes.

124. Chicken Pasties

Ingredients

- Minced chicken, 200 g
- Short crust pastry, 500 g (1 packet)
- Carrot, medium, 1
- Onion, small, 1
- Dried herbs
- Potato, medium, 100 g
- Black /white pepper, to taste

Directions

1. Preheat oven to 400 degrees F/ 200 degrees C / Gas mark 6.
2. In a saucepan (non-stick), brown the meat. To cover the meat halfway, add water and cook for 15 minutes. To extract extra liquid, drain the meat.
3. For 10 minutes, cook the potato, carrot & onion, drain well and chop into small bits. Stir in the mince. Flavor the meat & season with pepper & herbs as desired.
4. Using a saucer to cut 6 circles and roll out the pastry.
5. Divide the meat b/w the pastry rounds. Dampen the pastry corners, fold in half, and press together the corners to seal. Place it on a baking tray, then brush it with milk.
6. Bake in the middle of the oven for 25-30 mins.

CHAPTER 10

Vegetables

125. Low Potassium Potatoes

Two cooking methods are applied to reduce the potassium levels in potatoes

Ingredients

Method one:
- Potatoes - peeled and diced into 1cm cubes

Method two:
- Potatoes - peeled and cut into slices

Directions

Method one:
1. Wash and peel potatoes and dice into 1cm squares
2. Boil 10 times quantity of water as potatoes
3. Cook potatoes in boiling water until soft

Method two:
4. 'Twice boiled' potatoes
5. Wash and peel the potatoes and slice thinly.
6. Boil 4 times quantity of water as potatoes
7. Discard water and substitute with the same amount of new boiling water
8. Cook again, drain and take according to your allowance

126.Ratatouille

Ingredients

- Onion, 2 cups
- Eggplant, 1 medium
- Yellow bell pepper,1
- Zucchini squash, 2 cups
- Yellow crookneck squash, 3 cups
- Olive oil, 2 tbsp
- Tomatoes, 1 cup
- Parmesan cheese, grated, 8 tbsp canned
- Carrots, 2 medium
- Onion, 2 cups
- Eggplant, 1 medium
- Green bell pepper, 1
- Garlic, 4 cloves
- Red bell pepper, 1
- Fresh oregano, 1 tbsp
- Fresh rosemary, 1 tbsp
- Fresh sage, 1 tbsp
- Fresh basil, 1 tbsp
- Fresh thyme, 1 tbsp
- Black pepper, 1 tbsp

Directions

1. Cut the onion, eggplant, peppers, squash, and carrots into thin slices. Finely chop the cloves of garlic. Adding the Olive oil, ginger, black pepper, herbs, and carrots in a big saucepan, sauté.
2. introduce the remaining vegetables, except the tomatoes, then Fry for 2 minutes.
3. stir regularly and Fry well for 10 to 15 minutes or till the veggies are half tender.
4. put in parmesan and cheese tomatoes and coat well.
5. cook on reduced heat covered for around ½ an hour. Serve immediately.
6. Ratatouille can be served as a side dish or incorporate any type of pasta

127. Sauté Potatoes

Ingredients

- Reduced potassium potatoes 8oz
- Pepper ¼ tsp
- Margarine 1oz

Directions

1. Cook potatoes to decrease potassium given in Lo Potassium Potatoes
2. Cut the boiled potatoes into thin slices
3. Heat margarine till melted in a frying pan
4. Put in sliced lo potassium potatoes and sauté until well golden browned
5. Season with pepper

128. Savory Corn Pudding

Ingredients

- Corn canned 2 cups
- 1% milk ½ cup
- Eggs 3
- Onion chopped ⅓ cup
- Butter melted, 1 tbsp
- Paprika, ¼ tsp
- Water ½ cup
- White/black pepper, 1 tsp
- Salt a pinch, optional

Directions

1. Heat the furnace to 350degreeF.
2. Mix all of the ingredients.
3. Put it into a greased 1 ½-quart casserole.
4. Place the casserole in a pan filled with hot water (1").
5. Bake for about 40-45 minutes, or until the knife inserted in the middle is clean.
6. Let it stand at room temperature for 10 minutes before serving

129. Shepherd's Pie for Vegetarians

Ingredients

- Lentils, 300g tin, water drained
- Chickpeas, 16oz can water drained
- Tomatoes, chopped, 400g can water drained
- Dried mixed herbs, 1 pinch
- Couscous, 250g
- Hard cheese, grated, 60g
- Paprika, 1 tsp
- Mixed frozen vegetables, 2 cups
- Ground black pepper to taste

Directions

1. Place the mixed frozen veggies in a pan of cold water, then bring them to a boil.
2. Cook for 5 minutes, rinse and drain. Meanwhile, put all the other ingredients into a pan & heat through, leaving the couscous & cheese for later use.
3. Add the cooked vegetables. Put it in an oven-resistant bowl.
4. Following the instructions on the box, cook the couscous and scatter over the bowl.
5. Sprinkle over the couscous with the cheese and bake until golden brown. Serve with toasted bread.

130. Garlic Rice

Ingredients

- Garlic chopped 2 cloves
- Vegetable oil 2 tsp
- Long-grain white rice 100g
- Onion minced 1
- Chili pepper minced 1
- Stock cube ½ (reduced salt)
- Tomato chopped 1

Directions

1. Boil rice according to instruction.
2. To reduce extra starch, drain and clean it with cold water.
3. Adding the stock cube, put the rice to a boil again in 200 ml/3 quarters pint of cold water.
4. Mix the tomatoes, hot chili (onion & garlic, if desired), and vegetable oil.
5. Cook for 30 to 40 mins or before it absorbs the water.
6. Serve with a side salad.

131. Cheese and Onion Flan

Ingredients

- Skimmed milk, 150ml
- Spread, low fat, 1oz
- Flour, whole meal, 3oz
- vegetable fat, 2oz
- cheddar cheese 3oz
- egg 1
- salt a pinch
- cold water 3 tbsp.
- onion, sliced, 1
- black pepper as required
- dried mixed herbs a pinch
- 7" flan tin.

Directions

1. Heat the oven to Gas Mark 4/180 C/350 F/.
2. To make fine breadcrumbs, rub the low fat and white veg fat into the flour. To make a hard dough, add adequate cold water.
3. Thinly roll out and put in a flan tin. Prick the base of the flan case and place the onion on the base.
4. combine the egg, milk, cheese, and herbs & season with pepper. Pour it on the onion. For about 45 minutes, bake. Serve it hot or cold with a salad.

132. Golden Potato Croquettes

Ingredients

- Potatoes mashed 1lb
- Butter unsalted 1oz
- Milk ½ tbsp
- Black pepper ¼ tsp
- Salt ¼ tsp
- Egg, beaten, ½
- Breadcrumbs, fresh white, 3½ oz
- Olive oil, 3 tbsp for frying

Directions

1. Prepare the potatoes as given in Lo Potassium Potatoes
2. Mash the prepared lo potassium potatoes, milk butter, and seasoning in a bowl.
3. Make the croquette shape with your hand. Put aside.
4. Dip each croquette in the beaten egg and cover with breadcrumbs.
5. Heat a little olive oil in a frying pan. Put in the croquettes 4 to 5 at a time to rotate them easily.
6. Fry until golden and crisp on all sides.

133. Sesame Noodles with Tofu Stir-fry

Ingredients

- Olive oil 1 tbsp.
- Egg noodles 125g
- Garlic, crushed clove, 1
- Sesame oil, 1 tsp
- Soy sauce, reduced salt, 1 tbsp.
- Tofu, plain drained 250g
- Onions, sliced, 3
- Broccoli, small head, ½
- Carrot cut into strips, 1
- Ginger fresh chopped 3cm
- Honey 1 tbsp.
- Ground black pepper, to taste

Directions

1. Break the tofu into 2 cm cubes and season with olive oil, garlic, and ginger. Put aside.
2. Boil the noodles. Soak the noodles in ice water to keep them from sticking, drain & toss in sesame oil.
3. Boil the broccoli and carrots in plenty of unsalted water for five mins, drain and rinse again with cold water.
4. Heat a nonstick wok/frying pan, stir-fry for 2 to 3 minutes, and include the marinated tofu. Also include the broccoli, carrots, and 1 tbsp of water. Cover with a lid & steam till the tofu is cooked for 4-5 minutes, incorporating the onions at the end.
5. In a cup, add together the soy sauce & honey. Place the noodles on the plate adding the soy mixture. Toss well while it's all hot.
6. Add black pepper to season. Immediately serve.

134.Veggie Strata

Ingredients

- Slices sourdough bread,7 slices, ½-inch thick
- Unsalted margarine, 1tbsp
- Onion, 1 cup
- Red bell peppers, 1 cup
- Fresh spinach leaves, 15
- Raw mushrooms, 1 cup

- Large eggs, 7
- Half & half creamer, 1-¾ cup
- Worcestershire sauce,1 tsp
- Tarragon vinegar, ¼ cup
- Tabasco® hot sauce, 1 tsp
- Black pepper,½ tsp
- Sharp cheddar cheese, 1 oz. Shredded

Directions

1. Split the bread into little squares. Place it on the baking tray and bake it at 225 ° F for 15 minutes. Switch them over and bake for 15 more minutes, or until dry and crisp.
2. Dice the mushrooms, bell peppers, and onion.
3. Melt the margarine and sauté mushrooms, red peppers, and onions in a shallow saucepan.
4. Grease a baking dish (9-inch square) with the cooking spray. Spread half the bread squares in a single layer in the dish and sprinkle with half of the veggie mixture. Place this layer with the spinach leaves.
5. With the leftover bread and vegetables on top, create a second sheet.
6. Eggs, half & half creamer, vinegar, Worcestershire sauce, black pepper, and chili sauce are combined. Pour uniformly over the bread.
7. Cover with the plastic wrap and refrigerate for around 1 hour or overnight.
8. Bring strata at room temperature by making them stand outside the refrigerator for 20 minutes.
9. Heat the furnace to 325 ° F. Take the plastic wrap off and place it on for 50 minutes in the oven.
10. Remove it from the oven and spread the cheddar cheese on top. Bake for another 10 minutes or until the knife comes out clean when inserted in the middle.
11. Cut into nine squares and serve hot.

135. Low Potassium Vegetables

Ingredients

- · Root Vegetables - quantity as required

Directions

1. Select root vegetables that have naturally low potassium. A renal dietitian can offer you a list of appropriate vegetables.
2. Wash and peel the vegetables
3. Cut into small bits and put in a large pot for boiling.
4. Pour four times the volume of fresh boiling water as the vegetables.
5. Cover and put on a high flame.
6. Boil the water and then decrease the flame and simmer till veggies are fully cooked.
7. Drain and portion out your vegetable margin

136.Garlic Potato Mash

Ingredients

- Potato of low potassium, boiled, 9oz
- Garlic, crushed, 1 large clove
- Yogurt, plain, 1 tbsp
- Sour cream, 1 tbsp

Directions

1. Prepare low potassium potatoes (method given in recipes).
2. Add crushed garlic, sour cream and yogurt.
3. Mash it well and serve

137.Tempeh Pita Sandwiches

Ingredients

- Pita bread, 2 pieces, 6-inch size
- Mayonnaise, 4 tsp
- Onion, 1 small
- Balsamic vinegar, 2 tbsp
- Tempeh, 8 oz
- Sesame oil, 2 tbsp
- Bell pepper, red, 1
- Mushrooms, ½ cup

Directions

1. Cut the tempeh into 12 pieces. Thinly slice the bell pepper, the mushroom and the onion.
2. Heat 1 tbsp of sesame oil in a large skillet over medium heat. Place in sliced tempeh and fried on each side for 3 to 4 minutes until golden. Cook for one minute after incorporating balsamic vinegar; turn over and cook for one more minute. Take the tempeh out of the skillet.
3. Add the remaining sesame oil to the skillet and set it to low heat. Put in the bell pepper, onion and mushrooms and sauté until soft.
4. Break the pita in half and expand it to form an entrance. Spread 1 tsp of mayonnaise in half. Have ¼ of the mixture of vegetables and three slices of tempeh per half of the pita. Serve instantly

138.Potato Wedges

Ingredients

- Potatoes, 4
- Oregano dried 1 tsp
- Chili powder ½ tsp
- Paprika 2 tsp
- Vegetable oil 1 tbsp.
- Black pepper to taste

Directions

1. Heat oven to the mark of Gas 7/425oF/220oC.
2. Peel and cut the potatoes into small wedges.
3. Put them in a pan of cold water and carry them to a boil.
4. Boil and rinse after fifteen minutes.
5. Grease a baking sheet with oil.
6. Blend the paprika, oregano, and chili powder (if used) in a container.
7. Add the mix to potatoes & toss to coat.
8. assemble the wedges on a baking tray on a single sheet.
9. Cook until browned for 20 to 30 mins or until done.

139. Fragrant Rice with Coriander

Ingredients

- White rice, 3 oz
- Lemongrass, 1 stick, slit several times
- Coriander seeds, 2 tsp

Directions

1. Prepare your rice normally but add the coriander seeds and lemongrass to the boiling water.
2. When the rice is prepared, remove the lemongrass stick and serve.

140. Eggplant Casserole

Ingredients

- Eggplant 1 large
- Onion, finely chopped ½ cup
- Lean ground turkey 1 pound
- Vegetable oil 2 tbsp
- Green pepper, chopped ½ cup
- Plain bread crumbs 2 cups
- Egg, slightly beaten 1 large

- Red pepper, optional ½ tsp

Directions

1. Heat oven to 350 F.
2. Boil, drain & mash the eggplant.
3. Heat oil; put in ground turkey, onion & green pepper. Sauté until fried.
4. Mix in the eggplant, bread crumbs, and egg well.
5. Add, if required, red pepper to taste.
6. Bake for up to 30 to 45 mins in a casserole dish. Serve hot.

141. Easy Baked Green Beans

Ingredients

- Top cracker crumbs, 1 ½ cups, unsalted
- Margarine, 4 tbsp, unsalted
- Green beans, whole, 2 cans, drained and rinsed
- Fresh mushrooms, ½ cup, sliced
- Onion, 1 small, chopped
- Paprika, 1 tsp
- Black pepper, coarse, ¼ tsp

Directions

1. Heat oven to 350°F.
2. Combine mushrooms, green beans, black pepper, onion, and paprika.
3. Place in a baking casserole pan that is greased.
4. On the bean mixture, spread cracker crumbs and drizzle margarine.
5. Bake for about 30 to 35 minutes.

142. Vegan Provolone Cheese Sandwiches

Ingredients

- Sandwich rolls, 2, whole-grain
- Olive oil, 1 tbsp
- Red bell peppers, 2 medium
- Dahiya cheese, provolone-style, 4 slices
- Vegan cheese, 8
- Basil leaves, fresh

Directions

1. Wash and dry the red peppers with a towel of paper. Ignite two burners in the center of the stove. Place each of the peppers on the burners, using tongs. As one side begins to appear black, turn the peppers with tongs. Keep turning and cooking until all the peppers have blackened. It's going to take about 5-7 minutes.
2. Put the peppers in a paper bag with the help of tongs, cover. Put it aside for 5 to 8 minutes.
3. In the meanwhile, split all rolls in half lengthwise.
4. Pour the olive oil into a small bowl. Brush the oil inside of each sandwich bun.
5. Arrange 2 slices of Dahiya cheese on the bottom half of each roll. Place in a toaster oven. Toast until the cheese appears to melt. Take the rolls out of the toaster and put them aside.
6. Taking the red peppers out of the bag. Get rid of the blackened exterior pepper skin with your fingertips.
7. Remove the pepper stem and break open peppers to discard the seeds and any excess water with the paper cover. Cut the peppers in half.
8. Arrange two half-peppers on each half roll to make a sandwich, spread the fresh basil leaves and top with the other half roll.

143. Fresh Tofu Spring Rolls

Ingredients

- Medium red onion, ½
- Firm tofu, 16 oz
- Leaves romaine lettuce, 12
- Medium carrots, 2
- Ground cumin, ½ tbsp
- Granulated garlic, ½ tbsp
- Olive oil, 1 tbsp
- Rice wrappers, 12 for
- spring rolls
- Sea salt, ¼ tsp
- Black pepper, ½ tsp

Directions

1. Wash and dry the lettuce, then split each one in half lengthwise. Slice in daikon-style carrots. Cut the onion as well. Set aside.
2. Boil six cups of water and put it away to soak the rice wrappers for later.
3. Rinse and pat the tofu to dry. Break it into 12 slices, each roughly 4 inches long.
4. Assemble the tofu on a tray and season with half the cumin, sea salt, black pepper, and granulated garlic.
5. Heat the olive oil in a nonstick pan. Spread the tofu strips, seasoned side down, in the hot pan. Sprinkle the seasoning on the other side and cook for around 1 to 2 minutes until the bottom is lightly browned. Cook the other side until it is partially brown as well. Take the tofu out to cool on a pan.
6. Pour in the boiling water in a shallow, wide tub. In the hot bath, dip a rice wrapper. Put the wrapper on a large plate while it's slightly soft, and put 2 bits of the lettuce in the wrapper's center. Spoon 1- 2 tbsp of sliced onion and 2- 3 tbsp of carrot on top. On top of the vegetables, place one refrigerated strip of tofu.
7. Bend the sides in and then curl up the bottom and firmly curl it. Replicate all the rice wrappers, tofu strips, and vegetables in the process.
8. Chill in the fridge and serve cool, with ideally low-sodium dressing.

144. Spicy Buffalo Cauliflower Bites

Ingredients

- Cauliflower head, 1 medium
- All-purpose flour, ½ cup
- Water ½ cup
- Garlic powder 1 tbsp
- Black pepper 1 tsp
- Frank's red-hot buffalo wing sauce ½
- cup
- Ingredients for Lemon Dill Dip
- Sour cream
- Dried dill 1 tbsp
- Garlic powder 1 tbsp
- Lemon juice 2 tbsp

Directions

1. Preheat the stove oven to 450 degrees F. Spritz a nonstick baking tray lightly with cooking oil or lay on the parchment paper.
2. Combine the water, garlic powder, flour, and black pepper in a mixing bowl until well mixed.
3. Clean and cut the cauliflower into bite-sized bits. With the flour mixture, coat the cauliflower bits. Bake for 20 minutes on the baking sheet, toss it halfway.
4. Take the cauliflower out of the oven and apply the buffalo wing sauce. Allow baking until crispy, for 15-20 minutes.
5. Take from the oven and allow to rest before serving for 10 minutes. Serve hot with a dip of lemon dill.

145. Irish Mashed Potato

Ingredients

- Potatoes (cut into small pieces) 600g
- Onions 2 chopped
- Milk 1 or 2 tbsp.
- Ground black pepper

Directions

1. In a big pan of water, boil the potatoes until tender.
2. Drain the potatoes & mash with black pepper, milk, and spring onions.

146. Vegetables & Rice

Ingredients

- Rice, cooked, 2 ½ cups, salt-free
- Green peas, frozen, 1 10-oz package, cooked and drained
- Lemon juice, 1 tbsp
- Thyme, ½ tsp
- Onion, 1 medium, chopped
- Margarine, ¼ cup, unsalted

Directions

1. Fry chopped onion till tender in the margarine.
2. Add cooked rice, green peas, thyme, and lemon juice.
3. Cook, occasionally stirring, for 5 minutes.

147. Tofu Egg Fried Rice

Ingredients

- Yellow onion, 1 cup
- Extra-firm tofu, 1 cup
- Rice, 4 cups, cooked
- Garlic, 2 cloves
- Fresh ginger, 1 tbsp
- Medium carrots, 2
- Canola oil, 3 tbsp
- Green peas, ½ cup
- Cilantro, ½ cup
- Green onions, 2
- Large eggs, 6
- Dry mustard, ¼ tsp
- Soy sauce, reduced-sodium, 1 tbsp

Directions

1. Finely chop the ginger root and garlic. Cut the tofu and yellow onion into small squares. Slice the carrots. Chop the green onions and cilantro finely.
2. Beat the eggs well, and in a skillet, cook like an omelet. Break cooked eggs into small pieces and put them aside.
3. In a skillet, on medium flame, heat the oil. Stir in the yellow onion, ginger, garlic, carrots, tofu, peas, and dry mustard.
4. When carrots get soft, add the chopped eggs, rice, and soy sauce. Combine and take off from the heat.
5. Scatter with green onions and cilantro and serve.

148. Indian Chana Masala

Ingredients

- Medium onion, 1
- Canned chickpeas, 30 oz
- Canned tomatoes, 8 oz, diced, unsalted
- Garlic, 3 cloves
- Garam masala, 1 tsp
- Canola oil, 2 tbsp
- Chili powder, 1 tsp
- Fresh ginger, 1 tbsp
- Coriander powder, 1 tsp
- Fresh cilantro, ¼ cup
- Ground turmeric, 1 tsp
- Lemon wedges, 4

Directions

1. Cut the cilantro and onion finely; mince the ginger and garlic. Pour out and rinse the canned chickpeas thoroughly. In a big skillet, heat the oil and sauté ginger, onion, and garlic for 3 minutes.
2. Put in the tomatoes, and for another 3 to 4 minutes, keep cooking.
3. Add the coriander powder, garam masala, chili powder, and turmeric; Combine well and keep cooking for another 1 minute.
4. Put in the chickpeas and also ½ cup of water in the above. Let cook on low flame for around 10 to 15 minutes.
5. Garnish with lemon wedge and cilantro. Serve with rice, naan bread; if desired.

149. Garlicky Penne Pasta with Asparagus

Ingredients

- Asparagus, 1 pound
- Tabasco,¼ tsp, hot sauce
- Penne pasta, whole wheat, 8 oz, uncooked
- Parmesan cheese, ¼ cup shredded
- Olive oil, 2 tbsp
- Garlic, 6 cloves
- Butter, 2 tbsp
- Red pepper, 1/8 tsp, flakes
- Lemon juice, 2 tsp
- Black pepper, ½ tsp

Directions

1. Boil pasta without salt as per packet Instructions
2. Finely chop garlic. Chop 2-inch pieces of all asparagus.
3. On medium flame, heat butter and olive oil in a medium skillet. Add red pepper flakes and garlic and for 2-3 minutes sauté.
4. Add in pan the asparagus, lemon juice, Tabasco sauce, and black pepper and cook on medium for another 6 minutes until crisp and tender.
5. Empty pasta in a strainer and add to a bowl. Include asparagus and mix till well coated.
6. Top with shredded cheese
7. Serve immediately.

150. Baked Parmesan Yellow Summer Squash Rounds

Ingredients

- Yellow summer squash, medium-sized, 2
- Ground black pepper, a pinch
- Parmesan cheese freshly grated, ½ cup

Directions

1. Preheat the oven to 425 degrees F. Cover a baking sheet with foil and spray with nonstick cooking spray. Put an oven rack in the oven's central location.
2. Wash and clean the squash, then sliced it into ¼-inch thick slices each. Assemble the squash rounds with little to no room between them in the prepared tray.
3. Sprinkle the squash lightly with black pepper. Apply a thin coat of Parmesan cheese on each slice of the squash using a tiny spoon.
4. Bake 15 to 20 minutes, or until the Parmesan cheese melts and becomes golden brown lightly.
5. Serve immediately.

151. Vegetarian Pizza

Ingredients

- Roasted Pepper Tomato Sauce, 1 cup
- Readymade Pizza Dough (or make at home)
- Mushroom pieces, ⅓ cup
- Pineapple, ½ cup, tidbits
- Red onion, ½ cup
- Bell pepper, green, ½ cup
- Mozzarella, part-skim cheese, ½ cup, shredded
- Parmesan cheese, 2 tbsps., grated

Directions

1. Chop and Dice onion and bell pepper.
2. Heat oven to 425° F.
3. If not using readymade Prepare dough
4. Roll out dough to make two 12" pizza crusts.
5. Spread each pizza with ½ cup Tomato Sauce.
6. Scatter mushrooms, red onion, pineapple, and bell pepper on top.
7. Sprinkle Parmesan and mozzarella cheeses.
8. Bake in the oven for around 12-16 minutes till the top is browned and bubbly.

152. Easy Burrito

Ingredients

- Hot pepper sauce, ½ tsp
- Flour tortillas,2, burrito size
- Cooking spray, nonstick
- Green chiles, 3 tbsp, diced
- Ground cumin, ¼ tsp
- Eggs, 4

Directions

1. Grease a medium-size pan with a cooking spray and heat on medium heat.
2. Beat eggs in a bowl, including green chiles, hot sauce, and cumin. Pour beaten eggs into a hot skillet and fry and stir for 1 to 2 minutes till eggs are cooked.
3. In a separate skillet, heat tortillas on medium heat or place in microwave for 20 seconds. Put half of the egg mixture on each cooked tortilla and roll it up burrito style.

153. Vegetable Medley

Ingredients

- Cauliflower, 1 small
- Potato 9 oz,
- Olive oil 1 tbsp for frying
- Carrots 9 oz, thinly sliced
- Onions - 2 large, sliced
- Basil – chopped 1 tbsp
- Celery - 3 sticks
- Egg - 1 white and yolk separated
- Double cream - 1 tbsp
- Pepper - ¼ tsp
- For the sauce

- Milk 1 ½ cup
- Butter 1 ½ oz
- Cream cheese, ½ cup
- Flour 1 ½ oz

Directions

1. Cook low potassium potatoes and mush with a bit of margarine or butter, egg yolk, cream, and pepper.
2. Put aside to cool, then transfer to a big piping bag fitted with a nozzle.
3. Boil the celery, carrots, and cauliflower till soft and drain and rinse well.
4. Sauté onion in a bit of olive oil and assemble in a big serving dish.
5. Spread the cooked celery, carrots, and cauliflower on it and scatter the basil on top.
6. To prepare the sauce, heat the margarine in a pan till it melts and take off from the heat. Incorporate the flour until well mixed.
7. Slowly add the milk, place it back on medium heat and bring to a boil point, constantly stirring until it is thick.
8. Include the cream cheese mixing thoroughly, take off the heat. Dump the sauce on the cooked veggies.
9. Pipe potatoes in latticework over the veggies, Beat the egg white and brush on potatoes.
10. Bake at Gas mark 5/ 375 °F /190 °C, or till brown on top.

CHAPTER 11

Soups

154. Zucchini-Carrot Soup

Ingredients

- Onion, finely diced, 1medium
- Garlic, minced, 2cloves
- Veggie broth, no salt added, 2 Cup
- Oat milk 2 Cup
- Oat flour, coarsely ground, 3 Tbsp
- Basil,1 Tbsp
- Oregano, ½ Tbsp
- Zucchinis, grated, 2small
- Carrot, grated, 1medium
- Mrs. Dash seasonings & few shakes of the Bragg's Aminos

Directions

1. In a large saucepan, fry onion & garlic with a little broth or water till tender.
2. Mix in milk & broth & bring it to boil.
3. Whisk in oat flour (coarsely ground), oregano basil and a couple of sprinkles of Mrs. Dash.
4. Add the carrots & zucchini.
5. Decrease the heat & simmer for 5min till veggies are soft.
6. Mix often so the soup does not burn.
7. Add Bragg's Aminos, few shakes & enjoy.

155. Chicken Noodle Soup

Ingredients

- Unsalted butter, 1tbsp
- Minced onions, ¾ cup
- Celery, chopped, ½ cup
- Production of Chicken, 5cups
- Fried Chicken Breast, 8 oz
- Dry egg noodles, 2 cups
- Carrots sliced, 1 cup
- Oregano, grounded, ½ tsp
- Black Pepper, ground, ¼ tsp
- Basil ground, ½ tsp

Directions

1. All chicken is cooked and cut into tiny bits. Vegetables are cleaned and chopped.
2. Melt butter on medium heat. In the butter, cook the onion & celery until soft, about 5 minutes. Add in the chicken stock and all chicken, noodles, carrots, pepper, oregano, and basil. Just take it to a boil. Decrease the flame and let simmer for 20 minutes or so. Serve hot.

156. Roman Soup Jar

Ingredients

- Black olives, reduced-sodium, 3 large
- Garlic n herb seasoning, blend, ½ tbsp
- Black pepper, ½ tsp
- Red pepper flakes, 1/8 tsp
- Coleslaw mix, ½ cup
- Chickpeas, canned (no salt added), ⅓cup
- Ricotta cheese 1 tbsp
- Olive oil, extra virgin, 1 tsp
- Bell pepper and onion strips, frozen or fresh, ½ cup

Directions

1. Cut the slices of black olives. Rinse the chickpeas.
2. Layer all the ingredients in a 16-oz jar.
3. Cook to eat, refrigerate till serving.
4. Take the container from the fridge 15min before eating.
5. To blend, add 5oz of the boiling water into the container, close the lid tightly and shake. Let Ingredients sit for 2 min in the unopened pot.
6. Serve contents of jar in a large, deep bowl.

157. Mushroom Cream Soup

Ingredients

- Unsalted butter, 3tbsp
- Onion/shallot, Finely minced, ¼cup
- Mushrooms, finely minced, ¼cup
- All-purpose flour, 2 ½tbsp
- Low-Sodium chicken broth, ½cup
- Unsweetened almond milk, ½cup
- Sea salt, Dash
- Pepper to taste

Directions

1. In a 10inch pan, melt butter over med heat. Add onion & sauté till soft.
2. Add in mushrooms, mix & cook for around 5min. Sprinkle the flour over veggies & let cook for a min or 2.
3. Mix in broth & "milk" then stir till smooth. Decrease to simmer & cook till thick, about 5min.

158. Pumpkin Soup Low Sodium

Ingredients

- Pumpkin puree, 1 can (15 oz)
- Onion, chopped, 1 small
- Veggie broth, unsalted, 2 cups
- Ground nutmeg, ¼ tsp
- Ground cinnamon, ½ tsp
- Ground pepper, ¼ tsp
- Water, divided, ¾ cup
- Skim milk, 1 cup

Directions

1. Add ¼cup of water to a wide saucepan and heat on moderate to boil. Add onion, then simmer for 3 minutes.
2. Add remainder water, vegetable broth, pumpkin puree, cinnamon, nutmeg, and pepper. When simmering, mix well. Decrease flame and leave for 5 minutes to simmer. Add milk & keep simmering for 10 min.

159. Easy Chicken Noodle Soup

Ingredients

- Chicken parts, 1pound
- Egg noodles, 1cup
- Red pepper, 1tsp
- Lemon juice, ¼cup
- Caraway seed, 1tsp
- Water, 3½cups
- Oregano, 1tsp
- Poultry seasoning, 1tbsp
- Sugar, 1tsp
- Garlic powder, 1tsp
- Celery, ½cup
- Onion powder, 1tsp
- Green pepper, ½cup
- Vegetable oil, 2tbsp
- Black pepper, 1tsp

Directions

1. Pour lemon juice on the chicken parts and wash after 15 mins.
2. Mix chicken, onion powder, poultry seasoning, garlic powder & water in a large pot. Also, add in black pepper, sugar, oregano, red pepper, vegetable oil, and caraway seed.
3. Cook for 30min or till chicken meat is tender.
4. Include the remainder Ingredients & simmer for an additional 15min. Dish up hot.

160. Turkey, Rice, and Mushroom Soup

Ingredients

- Onion, ½cup
- Garlic, 2cloves
- Turkey, cooked, 2cups
- Chicken broth, low-sodium, 5cups
- Red bell pepper, ½cup
- Carrots, ½cup
- Rice, uncooked, ½ cup

- Olive oil, 1tbsp
- Mushrooms, sliced & canned, 4 oz
- Bay leaves, 2
- Salt, ½tsp
- Black pepper, ¼tsp
- Herbal seasoning blend, ¼tsp
- Thyme, dried, 1-½tsp

Directions

1. Chop the onion, carrots & bell pepper. Shred the turkey. Mince garlic finely.
2. In a large pot, boil 1-¾ cups of broth over medium heat; add in the rice & bring to boil. Decrease the heat to medium-low. Simmer covered for 5min / till liquid is absorbed. Now put aside.
3. In a Dutch oven, heat the oil over medium-high heat. Include the bell pepper, garlic, onion & carrots. Sauté, mixing once a while.
4. Rinse & drain mushrooms; afterward, add to veggies.
5. Add remaining 3-¼cups broth, bay leaves, turkey, thyme, pepper, Mrs. Dash seasoning & salt to the pan. Cook until it's thoroughly heated, mix.
6. Take out bay leaves & add cooked rice in soup. Serve immediately.

161. Four Ingredient Vegetable Broth

Ingredients

- Chicken broth, 1can
- Corn drained & rinsed, 1can

- Beans drained & rinsed, 1can
- Diced tomatoes, 1can

Directions

1. In a medium pot, blend all the ingredients.
2. Cook over low heat.
3. Garnish if you want.

162. Cream of Chicken Asparagus Soup

Ingredients

- Cooked chicken, 2cups
- Rice, long grain blend, ¾ cups
- Carrots, 1cup
- Asparagus, 2cups
- Unsalted butter, ¼cup
- Onion, ½cup
- Garlic, 3cloves
- Thyme, ½tsp
- Bay leaf, 1
- Pepper, fresh ground, ½tsp
- Nutmeg, ¼tsp
- Salt, ½tsp
- All-purpose flour, ½cup
- Chicken broth, low-sodium, 4cups
- Vermouth, extra dry, ½cup
- Almond milk, unsweetened & un-enriched, 4cups

Directions

1. Cook rice in ample water to reduce potassium content.
2. Take off the pan from heat & let the rice sit, for 15min, covered. Put aside & let cool.
3. Chop carrots, onion & asparagus coarsely. Nicely chop the garlic.
4. Melt butter in a deep pot, & sauté onion & garlic till fragrant. Put in the herbs, carrots & spices. Continue to cook on medium heat till soft.
5. Mix in the flour, simmer over low heat for almost 10min, mixing regularly.
6. Put in all of the vermouth & chicken broth. Mix till smooth by using the wire whisk.
7. Chop the cooked chicken into small pieces. Add the asparagus & chicken to the soup, then gradually add in almond milk. Now cook on low heat for 20min.
8. Mix in prepared rice before serving.

163. Vegetarian Soup

Ingredients

- Celery, ¾ cup
- Onion, ½cup
- Roma tomato, 1medium
- Green beans, fresh, 1cup
- Frozen corn, ½cup
- Carrots, ½cup
- Mushrooms, ½cup
- Veggie broth, low-sodium, 4cups
- Olive oil, 2tbsp
- Oregano leaves, dried, 1tsp
- Garlic powder, 1tsp
- Salt, ¼tsp

Directions

1. Remove strings & tips from the green beans, then cut them into pieces of 2inch. Chop onion, celery, tomato, carrots & mushrooms coarsely.
2. Heat large pot over medium heat, add olive oil & lightly fry onion & celery till tender.
3. Add-in remaining items & bring to boil. Lower heat to simmer it & cook for around 45-60min.

164. Gingerly Carrot Soup

Ingredients

- Garlic, minced, ½tsp
- Horseradish, ½tsp
- Canola oil, ½tsp
- Shallot, diced, 1
- Chicken stock, with Low-sodium, 2cup
- Carrots, 4diced
- Fresh ginger, sliced, 2tbsp

- Sugar, 1tsp
- Soy sauce, low-sodium, 4drops
- Sesame seed, roasted oil, ¼tsp
- Tofu, extra firm & Silken, 6oz
- White Vinegar, 2tsp

Directions

1. Add the oil, shallots, ginger, & carrots to a large saucepan.
2. Cook over medium flame until carrots appear to be soft. Add the horseradish & garlic, keep on cooking for 2min more.
3. Add in the chicken stock & crumbled tofu & cook over low heat for 15min. Include sugar, soy sauce & vinegar.
4. Puree soup with a blender. Serve soup & garnish sesame oil on every bowl.

165. Chicken and Cabbage Vegetable Soup

Ingredients

- Chicken breasts, chopped, 1½ pounds
- Cabbage, chopped into small pieces, ½ pound,
- Water, 10 cups
- Garlic, chopped, 1 clove
- Carrots, cut into small pieces, 2
- Tomato sauce, low-salt, ½ cup

- Onion, chopped, ½ cup
- Fresh cilantro, chopped, ½ cup
- Potato, cut into small pieces, 1
- Stalks celery, cut into small pieces, 3

Directions

1. Simmer in a large bowl, garlic, meat & water for ½ hr.
2. Add all the other Ingredients & cook over low heat till veggies are tender.

166. Nutritious Vegetable Soup

Ingredients

- Chicken broth, sodium-free, 32 oz
- Celery stalks, diced, 3
- Green beans, frozen, 2cups
- White rice, 1cup
- Onion, diced, 1
- Carrots, sliced, 2

Directions

1. Chop onion, celery & carrots coarsely.
2. To a 2-quart pot, add 2 cans of the salt-free chicken broth, carrots & frozen green beans.

For rice

3. Add the rice into the pot. Cook over low heat until carrots are soft.
4. For noodles
5. Add the noodles after the carrots are cooked & simmer over low heat until noodles are soft.

167. Ready Chicken Noodle Soup

Ingredients

- Rotisserie chicken, prepared, 1
- Chicken broth, low-sodium, 8 cups
- Onion, ½ cup
- Wide noodles, uncooked, 6 oz
- Celery, 1cup
- Carrots, 1cup
- Fresh parsley, 3 tbsp

Directions

1. Debone chicken and cut into bite-sized pieces. Take out the 4 cups broth for soup.
2. Into a large stockpot, pour in chicken broth, then bring to boil.
3. Dice the onion; slice the carrots & celery.
4. Add the veggies, noodles & chicken to the stockpot.
5. Boil it & cook for about 15min until noodles are cooked.
6. Sprinkle the chopped parsley on the top.

168. KIDNEY FRIENDLY POTATO SOUP

INGREDIENTS

- Potatoes, 3 medium
- Celery, chopped, ½cups
- Nondairy creamer,2tbsp
- Garlic, minced, 2 small cloves
- Chicken broth, Low-sodium, 2 ¼cups
- Onion, chopped, ¼cups
- Parsley, dried,½ tbsp

- Unsalted butter, 1 ¼tbsp
- Green onion, chopped, ½ cups

DIRECTIONS

1. In a skillet, melt the butter, add garlic, onion & celery. Sauté until tender.
2. Add the above to the large saucepan and the broth, nondairy creamer, demineralized potatoes & parsley.
3. Continue cooking over low flame for almost 20-30min.
4. Keep stirring & breaking up potatoes as it simmers. Now spoon out to a soup bowl & scatter it with green onion.

169. CHICKEN & VEGETABLE SOUP

INGREDIENTS

- Chicken boneless, 1pound
- Water, 3½cups
- Raw Onions, sliced, 1cup
- Green peas, frozen, ½cup
- Thyme, ½tsp
- Frozen corn, ½cup
- Black pepper, 1tsp

- Okra, frozen, ½cup
- Basil, ½tsp
- Carrots, diced & frozen, ½cup

DIRECTIONS

1. Place the chopped boneless breast, thyme, black pepper, onions, basil & water in a large skillet. Cook on medium heat until chicken is slightly tender, about 15min.
2. Put in all the frozen veggies; simmer on low heat till chicken and veggies are tender.

CHAPTER 12

Desserts

170. Crème Brule

Ingredients

- Pineapple slices, 2 tinned, 3oz
- Double cream,5 fluid oz
- Egg, small, 1
- Vanilla essence, ½ tsp
- Castor sugar, 2 oz

Directions

1. Preheat your oven to Gas Mark 2/150C.
2. Pat pineapple till dry with kitchen paper, now coarsely chop & place in the bottom of two greased ramekin dishes (about 8-9 cm diameter).
3. Heat cream lightly till it starts to bubble around the boundaries, but does not boil.
4. Add half of the sugar to the egg in a large mixing bowl & whisk till well incorporated. Slowly mix in the cream; afterward, stir in vanilla essence.
5. Pour batter over pineapple, leaving a 1 cm gap to the rim of the dish.
6. Put ramekins in a shallow baking dish filled with boiling water to a depth of 3 cm/ ¾ the ramekin depth.
7. Place in the oven for 25 to 30min or till the custard's set. Take out & cool. Chill for an hour or overnight.
8. Bring grill to its hottest position.
9. Sprinkle remainder sugar equally over the top of the custard. Brown & bubble under the grill. Chill for an hr. before serving.

171. Apple Crumble

Ingredients

- Cooking apples, peeled cored & thinly sliced, 18oz
- Plain flour, 4oz
- Rolled oats, 3oz
- Brown sugar, 3oz
- Ground cinnamon, 2 tsp
- Butter or hard margarine, 3oz

Directions

1. Preheat your oven to Gas mark 5/190C.
2. In a small oven-safe pie dish, arrange sliced apples & sprinkle with 1 oz of sugar. Mix flour, cinnamon, oats & remaining sugar altogether in a bowl.
3. Cut the butter into small cubes. Then add oats & rubbing with your fingers till the mixture resembles crumbs.
4. Sprinkle that crumble mixture equally over the fruit.
5. Put in the oven for 40-50min until the crumble becomes golden brown & fruit juices start boiling at the side.

172. Vanilla Ice Cream

Ingredients

- Egg yolks, 3
- Caster sugar, 4oz
- Milk, low phosphate, 300ml
- Vanilla essence, 1tsp
- Double cream, 150ml

Directions

1. Place sugar & the egg yolks in a large bowl & beat with a wooden spoon's help till the mixture becomes creamy & pale.
2. Lightly heat the milk, then add vanilla essence & slowly add it to sugar & eggs, mixing well.
3. Sieve the mixture into the bowl over a pan with simmering water.
4. Simmer on a gentle heat for almost 30min, stirring continuously, till the mixture gets thick enough to be coated around the spoon's back. Don't allow it to boil.
5. Leave the mixture to cool down; afterward, mix in the cream & transfer into a shallow ice container.
6. Put in freezer for minimum 2-3hrs. The ice cream must be stirred quite a few times while freezing the process to prevent crystals' formation.

173. Jam Turnovers

Ingredients

- Puff pastry, 9 oz
- Jam, 9 oz
- Double cream, 4tbps
- Egg white, 1
- Castor sugar, 1 oz

Directions

1. Roll out pastry to a thickness of ¼inch. By using a cutter, cut it into 4-inch rounds. A saucer will help if you do not have a cutter.
2. Spread each round till slightly oval, about 5x4inches. Wet the edges with a wet pastry brush.
3. In the center of each pastry, put a little jam. Then fold over & seal firmly. Now brush it with egg white & scatter it with caster sugar.
4. Put the sugar side up on an oiled baking sheet & bake for around 15-20min in the hot oven (Gas mark 7, 220°C, 425°F)
5. Serve it with double cream.

174. Cinnamon Rice Pudding

Ingredients

- Double cream, 300ml
- Pudding rice, 4oz
- Water, 300ml
- Sugar, 75g (3oz)
- Whole milk, 300ml
- Vanilla extract, 1tsp
- Ground cinnamon, 1tsp

Directions

1. Place all Ingredients leaving cinnamon & vanilla essence into the pan & stir well.
2. Heat over med-low heat for almost 1hr.
3. Stir often just to ensure that rice isn't sticking to the bottom of the pan.
4. Stir in vanilla essence & also cinnamon to taste, once the rice is cooked. Continue warming thoroughly for about 10min.

175. Chia Pudding

Ingredients

- Chia seeds, ½cup
- Plant-based milk, 1 ½cups
- Vanilla extract, 1tsp
- Maple syrup, 2 tbsp

Directions

1. Add all the ingredients to the mason jar. Mix well to combine.
2. Cover & chill for a minimum of 4hrs or overnight
3. Additions & Variations:
4. Chocolate: Add 2tbsp of the cocoa powder
5. Berry: Add frozen/ fresh mixed berries for topping
6. Higher Protein: Add nut/seed butter, nuts, or seeds. Substitute soy milk for rice milk.

176. Lemon Drizzle Cake

Ingredients

- Butter/margarine, low in salt, 225g
- Self-rising flour, sieved, 225g
- Eggs, 4
- Lemon juice, ½
- Caster sugar, 225g
- For the icing
- Icing sugar, 110g
- Lemon Juice, 1

Directions

1. Preheat your oven to 180oC or 350oF or Gas Mark 4.
2. The butter & sugar should be creamed till light and fluffy.
3. Eggs must be added 1 at a time and beating well in b/w.
4. Insert flour & carefully mix in. Add juice & lemon rind.
5. In the cake pan, dump the mixture into it. Bake till golden and cake bounces back when it's touched, for approx. 70 min.
6. Remove paper from the tin, now peel it off & allow it to cool.
7. Mix lemon juice with icing sugar & spill icing over the cake just to allow it to flow down its sides.
8. Sprinkle with the zest of lemon.

177. Spiced Baked Apple

Ingredients

- Bramley apple, 1
- Cinnamon, ½tsp
- Sugar, 1tsp

Directions

1. Core center of apple & place it on a microwavable plate.
2. Combine cinnamon & cloves with sugar and spoon into the middle of the apple.
3. Cook for 2-3min / till tender, in micro on med strength.

178. Fruit Flan

Ingredients

- Flan case, 1 Sponge
- Fruit cocktail, 16oz tin
- Red quick jelly, 1 packet

Directions

1. Drain fruit juice out of a can & discard it.
2. Put a case of flan on a flat plate and arrange the fruit. You have to follow the instructions on the package for making up swift jelly.
3. Leave it to cool & spill it over the fruit after a couple of mins. Leave it to set.
4. Use a spoonful / 2 of cream to serve it.

179. Pineapple and Ginger Meringues

Ingredients

- Whipping cream, half-fat, 8oz
- Meringue nests, 4
- Pineapple chunks, juice drained, 8oz can
- Chopped ginger syrup, 2oz stem

Directions

1. On separate serving plates/pans, organize meringue nests.
2. In crème Fraiche, mix in diced ginger.
3. With the ginger-crème Fraiche, fill meringue nests & top with chunks of the pineapple.

180. Mini Pineapple Upside Down Cakes

Ingredients

- Unsalted butter, melted, 3tbsp
- Brown sugar, packed, ⅓cup
- Pineapple slices, unsweetened, 12 canned
- Cherries, fresh & cut into halves n pitted, 6
- Sugar, 2/3 cup
- Fat-free milk, 2/3 cup
- Canola oil, 3 tbsp
- Egg 1
- Lemon juice, 1tsp
- Vanilla extract, ½tsp
- Cake flour, 1-⅓cups
- Baking powder, 1-¼ tsp
- Salt, ¼ tsp

Directions

1. Pour the butter into a muffin tray with 12servings. Square pan, just for baking.
2. Sprinkle each of the segments with a little bit of brown sugar.
3. Press 1 slice of pineapple in each segment to make a cup shape. Putting one half of the cherry (cut side will be facing up) & set aside in every pineapple slice center.
4. Beat milk, sugar, egg, oil, and extracts in a large bowl till well blended. Combine baking powder, flour & salt; beat in sugar mixture till smooth. In a muffin tin, mix in the prepared batter.
5. For 35-40min, bake at 350° until a toothpick emerges clean. Now Invert the muffin pan immediately & slip cooked cakes into the serving plate. If necessary, you can use a butter knife / tiny spatula around the edges to carefully release them from the tray. Serve warm.

181. PUMPKIN STRUDEL

INGREDIENTS

- Unsweetened pumpkin, sodium-free, 1½ cups canned.
- Grated nutmeg, ⅛ tsp
- Vanilla extract, 1 tsp
- Sugar, 4 tbsp
- Ground cinnamon, ½ tsp
- Butter, unsalted, melted, 4 tbsp, (½ stick)
- Phyllo dough, 12 sheets (if frozen, then follow package Instructions for defrosting)

DIRECTIONS

1. Preheat the oven to 380° F, and then arrange the oven rack in the oven center.
2. Pour the canned pumpkin, vanilla extract, nutmeg, ½ tbsp of cinnamon, and 2 tbsp of sugar in a medium-sized mixing bowl, mix until well-mixed.
3. Coat a nonstick medium baking tray with butter with the help of a pastry brush. Lay a flat single phyllo dough sheet on a clean work table and then apply butter to it. Stack buttered phyllo sheets one by one on them, brushing each phyllo sheet with the melted butter. (Save a little quantity of melted butter to brush the top of the strudel.) Keep covered the remaining phyllo sheets with plastic wrap until ready for use.
4. Spread the mixture on one of the stack's longer sides evenly when all the 12 sheets are done. Now begin to roll from the filling end to the empty end and make sure that the seam-side is downwards.
5. Transfer the roll seam-side downward on the greased sheet tray and brush with the remaining butter.
6. Mix the remaining sugar and cinnamon in a small bowl. Then spread it on the sides and also on the top of the strudel.
7. Place the oven's center rack until lightly toasted or golden brown, about 12 to 15 minutes.
8. Now take out the baked strudel from the oven and then let the toasted strudel rest for about 5 to 10 min.
9. At last, let the center settle, slice with a sharp knife, and serve.

182. Lemon Meringue Pie

Ingredients

Pie Filling.
- Egg yolks, raw, 6.
- Cornstarch,⅓ cup.
- Water, 1 ½ cups.
- Salt,¼ tsp.
- Butter, unsalted,1 ¼ tbsp.
- Lemon juice,½ cup.
- Lemon zest 2 tbsp.
- Sugar,1 ⅓ cup.

Meringue Topping.
- Egg whites,6.
- Cream of tartar, 1 pinch.
- Sugar,2 ½ tbsp.
- Use either a pie shell or graham cracker crust.

Directions

For the lemon filling:
1. Heat the oven to 375 F.
2. Put the egg yolks in a medium-sized mixing bowl and put aside. Combine cornstarch, water, salt, and sugar in a medium saucepan. Now whisk to blend. Turn on the stovetop to medium heat and take the mixture to a boil, stirring it frequently. Boil for about 1 to 2 min.
3. Remove the water and sugar mixture off the heat and slowly add the heated mixture to the yolks. Stir until they are combined in an even mixture. Then return the sugar- egg-water mixture to the same pan. Now turn the heat down to low and cook, stirring continuously for 1 to 2 additional min.
4. Remove from heat and then gently mix in butter, zest, and lemon juice until they are well combined. This may look lumpy, but stirring constantly will bring everything beautifully together.
5. Dump this mixture into the prepared pie shell and progress to make the meringues.

For the meringue:
6. Put the cream of tartar and egg whites in the bowl of a stand mixer, with the whisk attachment fitted. Beat the egg whites to form soft peaks and then slowly add the sugar. Now continue beating till stiff peaks are formed, around 2 to 3 min. Stiffer peaks will make a better meringue pie crust.
7. Top your meringue on the lemon filling that was previously in the pie shell. Top with meringue when filling is still hot, as it will help to stick better. Make sure to cover the filling with the meringue completely.
8. Bake until meringue is golden or for 8 to 12 minutes. Remove from oven and cool. The pie must be cooled completely before slicing.

183. Cherry Brown Butter Bars

Ingredients

Crust
- Butter, unsalted, melted, ¾ cup.
- Sugar,2/3 cup.
- Flour, 2 cups+2 tbsp
- Salt, 1/8 tsp.
- Vanilla extract, ½ tsp.
- Cherry Filling and Creamy Top
- Butter, unsalted, diced, 1 cup.
- Eggs, 3
- Sugar, 2/3 cup.

- Salt, 1/8 tsp.
- Flour, ½ cup.
- Vanilla extract, 1 tsp
- Almond, 1 tsp extract
- Cherries 4 cups, pitted & tossed with 2 tsp flour

Directions

1. Heat oven to 375°F and then line with parchment paper a 13 x 9-inch baking dish.
2. Mix melted butter, vanilla, and sugar in a medium bowl with the help of a spatula. Add salt and flour, then stir until well combined. Flatten the dough equally into the bottom of the lined baking dish and bake till the crust is slightly puffed and golden for about 18 minutes. Remove from oven to a wire rack and then let the crust cool in the pan.
3. To make the filling, cook butter in a big saucepan on medium heat, stirring continuously till it foams, turns transparent and then turns to a deep brown for about 6 minutes. Transfer browned butter to a glass measuring cup and cool slightly. Beat together eggs, salt, and sugar, in a medium mixing bowl. Include flour and extracts, then mix until smooth. Slowly whisk the browned butter in; whisk the mixture until completely incorporated.
4. Assemble cherries on the cooled crust, then carefully pour filling equally over fruit. Bake for around 30 minutes, till filling, is golden and puffed, inserting a toothpick in the center as it comes out clean. Completely Cool the bars in the pan on a wire rack. With care, lift parchment to transfer the bars from the pan now place on a cutting board. Cut them into squares with a serrated knife. Store bars in an airtight container in the refrigerator.

CHAPTER 13

Smoothies and Drinks

184. Italian lemonade – a unique renal friendly beverage

Ingredients

- Fresh basil, washed & stemmed 1 bunch
- Sugar, 2 cups
- Water, 1 cup
- Lemon juice, about 12 to 15 lemons, 2 cups
- Sparkling /cold water, 2 cups

Directions

1. For simple basil syrup: In a pot, combine basil, 1cup water, & 2cups sugar & simmer till the sugar is melted, 5min. Cool, strain & store in the fridge till ready to use.
2. Blend the simple basil syrup, lemon juice & 2cups of cold /sparkling water in the pitcher for the lemonade. Chill till ready to serve.

185. Pineapple Coconut Turmeric Smoothie

Ingredients

- Coconut milk, can, 1 Cup
- Almond milk, unsweetened, 1 Cup
- Pineapple, diced, 2 Cups
- Ginger, peeled & grated, 1 Tbsp
- Turmeric powder, 1 tsp

Directions

1. Put all the ingredients in the blender. Blend till smooth.
2. For a thicker drink, take less almond milk & more coconut milk. Adjust the thickness as desired.

186. Renal friendly Indian masala tea

Ingredients

- Water, 6cups
- Heavy whipping cream, 1.5 cup
- Rice milk, 2.5 cup
- Black tea leaves, 2 tbsp
- Cinnamon, 2 sticks
- Black peppercorns, 2
- Whole cloves, 10
- Cardamom pods, 6
- Star anise, 2–3
- Brown sugar, ½ cup (or to taste)

Directions

1. In a large saucepan, add the spices to a cup of water. Boil and take off from the heat; let stand for 5-20min, depending upon how strong spicy flavor you desire.
2. Add rice milk & cream to the spiced water. Bring it all to a boil & take off from the heat.
3. Add tea leaves to milk & reheat to a simmer for 2 minutes to get the taste you desire.
4. Sieve into the pot. Serve. Adding the sugar to taste.

187. Lime Cranberry Apple Spritzer

Ingredients

- Lime 1 zest
- Fresh/frozen cranberries, 2 bags (12oz)
- Fresh lime juice (almost 5 limes), 2/3 cup
- Honey, 3Tbsp
- Apple juice, 4cups
- Chilled seltzer water, 1bottle

Directions

1. Zest a lime: Make lime zest, using a veggie peeler to take-off strips. Just get the zest portion, as that has all the flavor.
2. Juice all the limes.
3. In a large pot, mix the cranberries, honey, lime zest &. Apple juice, take to boil.
4. Decrease to simmer & cook till all the berries have popped, about 15min.
5. Sieve the mixture through a fine-mesh strainer, squeezing the berries to excerpt as much juice as possible.
6. Cool to room temperature; afterward, transfer lime cranberry juice into a juice container or a jar with a fitted lid.
7. Add in lime juice & whisk to combine.
8. Stock it in the refrigerator.
9. Makes five cups of juice.
10. For 1 spritzer: Pour ¼cup lime cranberry juice into a tall glass & add in ½cup iced seltzer.

188. Party Punch

Ingredients

- Liquid pineapple concentrate, ½cup
- Ginger ale, diet, 1 liter
- Sherbet, lime-flavored, 1 pint

Directions

1. Pour the ginger ale into a large mixing bowl/punch bowl.
2. Add the pineapple concentrate & stir.
3. Add the sherbet with the scoop.
4. Serve when the sherbet begins to melt.

189. Chocolate kidney-friendly Smoothie

Ingredients

- Almond milk, 1 cup
- Chocolate-flavored whey protein, 2scoops
- Ice, 2cups
- Cinnamon, ground, ¼tsp
- Nutmeg, Pinch

Directions

1. In a blender, mix all the ingredients, excluding cinnamon, on high till smooth, approximately 1 to 2 minutes.
2. Decorate with whipped cream and add a dash of cinnamon to garnish.

190. Berry yogurt smoothie

Ingredients

- Plant-based yogurt, unsweetened, ¾ cup
- Mixed berries, frozen, 1.5cup
- Maple syrup, 1tsp
- Non-dairy milk/water to thin, ¼cup

Directions

1. Add in all the items in a blender. Blend till smooth; add almond milk /water as required to get the desired thickness. Add maple syrup for a taste.

191. Blissed Watermelon Drink

Ingredients

- Watermelon, 2cups
- Cucumber, peeled & sliced, 1medium
- Squeeze of lime
- Ice cubes
- Mint sprigs, 2 leaves only
- Celery stalk, 1

Directions

1. Blend all the ingredients in a power blender till smooth.
2. Pour in tall glass & serve.

192. FOREVER LEMONADE

INGREDIENTS

- Water, 2-½cups
- Sugar, 1-¼cups
- Lemon, finely shredded, ½tsp
- Lemon, fresh, 1-¼cups
- Ice cubes

DIRECTIONS

1. Mix water & sugar substitute/sugar. In a med pot, over med heat, until sugar's dissolved. Take it off from heat & cool for 20min.
2. Put in juice & citrus peel to the sugar mix. Pour out into pitcher or jar; chill covered.
3. To make 1 glass of lemonade, mix the base 3oz & water 3oz in a glass filled with ice. Mix n enjoy it. The leftover base can be frozen in the ice trays & used as ice.

193. FLAVORFUL ORANGE COFFEE

INGREDIENTS

- Coffee-Mate Powder, 1 cup
- Orange peel, dried, ½ tsp
- Instant coffee, ½ cup
- Sugar, ¾ cup

DIRECTIONS

1. In a dry blender, blend all ingredients till powdered.
2. Add two heaped tsp of the coffee mix in a mug for each serving & add boiling water.

194. Peachy Delight

Ingredients

- Honey, 1tbsp
- Almond milk, unsweetened & vanilla flavored, 1 cup
- Raspberries, frozen, 1cup
- Peach, pit removed & sliced, 1 medium
- Silken tofu, ½cup

Directions

1. Put all Ingredients in a blender till smooth.
2. Pour in a tall glass.

195. Blue Lagoon Smoothie

Ingredients

- Blueberries, frozen, 1cup
- Splenda, 8packets
- Protein powder, 6tbsp
- Ice cubes, 8
- Apple juice, 14oz

Directions

1. In the blender, blend all Ingredients & mix till smooth.

196. Pro Pineapple Smoothie

Ingredients

- Pineapple sherbet, ¾ cup
- Vanilla flavored Whey protein powder, 1scoop
- Water, ½cup

Directions

1. Add pineapple sherbet, whey protein powder & water in a blender.
2. Mix for 30-45sec; serve immediately.

197. Summery Cooler

Ingredients

- Ice, crushed, 1cup
- Seedless watermelon, cubes, 1cup
- Lime juice, 2tsp
- Sugar, 1tbsp
- Watermelon wedges, 2small (to garnish it)

Directions

1. Blend all Ingredients in the blender, excluding wedges separated for garnish & blend well for about 30sec.
2. Take it out into two med glasses, garnish it with wedges.

198. MIXED BERRY SMOOTHIE

INGREDIENTS

- Coldwater, 4 oz
- Mixed berries, fresh/frozen, 1 cup
- Ice cubes, 2
- Crystal Light, flavor enhancer drops, 1 tsp
- Cream topping, whipped, ½ cup
- Whey protein powder, 2 scoops

DIRECTIONS

1. Add the frozen berries, water, ice cubes and crystal light drops into a blender. Blend until mixed well & slushy.
2. Put in the protein powder & mix well
3. Put in the cream topping & mix well.

199. HEALTHY KIDNEY SMOOTHIE

INGREDIENTS

- Cucumber, peeled & sliced, ½ large
- Blueberries, fresh & frozen, 1 cup
- Cinnamon, 1 pinch
- Lime juice, fresh, a good squeeze
- Ice, 1 cup
- Coconut water, 1 cup
- Chia seeds, 1-2 tbsp

DIRECTIONS

1. In the power blender, add all Ingredients & secure the lid.
2. Turn on the machine & gradually increase speed to High.
3. Keep scraping sides of the blender with a spatula if necessary while processing.
4. Keep Blending for 60-90sec / until the desired thickness is reached.

200. Simple Blueberry Smoothie

Ingredients

- Blueberries, frozen, ¼ cup
- Rice milk, 1 cup
- Honey, 1 tsp
- Fresh mint, 1 sprig
- Ice cubes (just to obtain the desired thickness)

Directions

1. Puree rice milk, honey, blueberries, extra ice & mint in a blender. Pour in a tall glass.

CONCLUSION

The goal of stage 3 and 4 CKD treatment is to avoid further progression. There is no cure for any stage of chronic kidney disease, and you can't undo kidney damage.

But, further damage can easily be minimized when you're at stage 3. It is more difficult to avoid progression in CKD stages 4 and 5.

Good lifestyle improvement and self-management will help you live a healthy, long, fulfilling, pain-free life and do all the things you love and desire. It can also slow and stop the worsening of kidney disease, and it can even delay or stop kidney failure. Good self-management and lifestyle change start with:

- Eating the right type of food, according to your disease
- Managing other health risks that you may have
- Treating complications of kidney disease
- Managing or preventing heart disease

It is safe to say that by changing your lifestyle according to your disease and following your medical helper's guidelines, you can easily manage the disease from advancing.

Printed in Great Britain
by Amazon

58067910R00081